Competition Law in Montenegro

Competition Law in Montenegro

Mijat Jocović

This book was originally published as a monograph in the International Encyclopaedia of Laws/Competition Law.

Founding Editor: Roger Blanpain
General Editor: Frank Hendrickx
Volume Editors: Francesco Denozza & Alberto Toffoletto

Wolters Kluwer

Published by:
Kluwer Law International B.V.
PO Box 316
2400 AH Alphen aan den Rijn
The Netherlands
E-mail: international-sales@wolterskluwer.com
Website: lrus.wolterskluwer.com

Sold and distributed in North, Central and South America by:
Wolters Kluwer Legal & Regulatory U.S.
7201 McKinney Circle
Frederick, MD 21704
United States of America
Email: customer.service@wolterskluwer.com

Sold and distributed in all other countries by:
Air Business Subscriptions
Rockwood House
Haywards Heath
West Sussex
RH16 3DH
United Kingdom
Email: international-customerservice@wolterskluwer.com

ISBN 978-94-035-2282-1

e-Book: ISBN 978-94-035-2283-8
web-PDF: ISBN 978-94-035-2284-5

The Author

Mijat Jocović obtained his Bachelor's degree in Law from the School of Law, University of Montenegro, Montenegro, in 2003. He earned his Master's degree in Law in September 2007 from the Faculty of Law, the University of Belgrade, Serbia, in the field of business law. In March 2011, he defended his PhD thesis with honours at the Faculty of Law, University of Belgrade. He passed the bar exam in 2014.

On 1 February 2004, he started working at the Faculty of Economics of the University of Montenegro as a Teaching Assistant for the subjects Business Law and International Business Agreements. In 2012, he was promoted to Assistant Professor at the University of Montenegro for the subjects Business Law and International Business Agreements. In addition to these subjects, since 2012 he has been teaching Law and European Union institutions at the Faculty of Economics in Podgorica. In 2017, he was promoted to Associate Professor at the Faculty of Economics of the University of Montenegro. Since 2016, he has held the position of Vice-Dean.

In addition to his engagement with the University of Montenegro, Mijat Jocović has been hired as a legal advisor in various business law cases. As a consultant, he actively cooperates with law firms in Montenegro. He has participated as a member of working groups in the preparation of numerous laws in the field of business law. Mijat Jocović has presented papers and participated in numerous domestic and international conferences.

The Author

Table of Contents

List of Abbreviations

2006 Competition Act	Law on Protection of Competition (*Zakon o zaštiti konkurencije, Službeni list Crne Gore* 69/05)
AECPS	Agency for Electronic Communications and Postal Services
AEM	Agency for Electronic Media
Agency	Agency for Protection of Competition
CBM	Central Bank of Montenegro
CJEU	Court of Justice of the European Union
Competition Act	Law on Protection of Competition (*Zakon o zaštiti konkurencije, Službeni list Crne Gore* 44/2012)
EML	Electronic Media Law (*Zakon o elektronskim medijima, Službeni list Crne Gore* 046/10, 040/11, 053/11, 006/13, 055/16, 092/17)
EU	European Union
FRY	Federal Republic of Yugoslavia
GDP	Gross Domestic Product
ISA	Insurance Supervision Agency
JIS	Judicial Information System
KSCS	Kingdom of Serbs, Croats, and Slovenians
LAD	Law on Administrative Dispute (*Zakon o upravnom sporu, Službeni list Crne Gore* 054/16)
LCBM	Law on Central Bank of Montenegro (Zakon o Centralnoj banci Crne Gore, *Službeni list Crne Gore* 40/10, 46/10, 6/13, 70/17)
LEC	Law on Electronic Communications (*Zakon o elektronskim komunikacijama, Službeni list Crne Gore* 040/13, 056/13, 002/17)
LSAC	Law on State Aid Control (*Zakon o kontroli državne pomoći, Službeni list Crne Gore* 74/09, 57/11)
RDC	Radio Difuzni Centar

List of Abbreviations

R&D BED	Decree on Group Exemption of Horizontal Research and Development Agreements (*Uredba o grupnom izuzeću od zabrane horizontalnih sporazuma o istraživanju i razvoju, Službeni list Crne Gore* 13/14)
REA	Energy Regulatory Agency
SAA	Stabilisation and Association Agreement Between the European Communities and Their Member States, of the One Part, and the Republic of Montenegro, of the Other Part
Specialization BED	Decree on Group Exemption of Horizontal Specialization Agreements (*Uredba o grupnom izuzeću od zabrane horizontalnih sporazuma o specijalizaciji, Službeni list Crne Gore* 13/14)
TFEU	Treaty on the Functioning of the European Union, O.J. [2008] C 115/47.
Transfer Technology BED	Decree on Group Exemption of the Transfer of Technology Agreements (*Uredba o grupnom izuzeću od zabrane sporazuma o prenosu tehnologije, Službeni list Crne Gore* 59/14)
Vertical BED	Decree on Group Exemption of Vertical Agreements (*Uredba o grupnom izuzeću vertikalnih sporazuma od zabrane, Službeni list Crne Gore* 13/14)

General Introduction

§1. General Background of Montenegro

I. Geography and Climate

1. Montenegro (in Montenegrin: *Crna Gora*) is located in south-eastern Europe, on the Balkan Peninsula. The territory of Montenegro occupies approximately 13,812 km^2,[1] and the coastline is 293.5 km long.

2. Montenegro is bordered by Croatia (14 km long border) to the west, Bosnia and Herzegovina to the north (225 km), Serbia to the east (203 km), Albania to the south (172 km), and it is separated from Italy by the Adriatic Sea.

3. Montenegro is divided into three areas: the coastal, the central and the mountain region. The coastal area is the southernmost, narrow area (1–10 km wide) extending along the Adriatic Sea from Igalo in the west to the mouth of the river Bojana on the east. The summers are long and dry, and winters are short and mild.

4. The central area of the country consists of two parts. The first part is the mountain range that is literally looming over the coastline. This part of the country holds a record in Europe in terms of rainfall. In this area, there is the ancient capital of Montenegro – Cetinje. The second part of the central geographical area is plain. There is basin of Skadar Lake (national park), the fertile valley of the river Zeta, Bjelopavlići plain and Nikšić field. These are the places with the highest population density in Montenegro. The summer is extremely hot; the temperature reaches 40°C. The average winter temperature usually does not go below -5°C.

5. Mountain area occupies the northern part of the country. Here is sub-alpine climate, with cold, snowy winters and moderately warm summers.

1. Statistical data used in this section was collected from the webpage of the Statistical Office of Montenegro (available in English): https://www.monstat.org/eng/ (last accessed 5 Jul. 2019).

II. Population

6. Montenegro has a population of approximately 622,471. The largest city and capital of the country is Podgorica. Other major cities are Nikšić (central area), Bijelo Polje and Pljevlja (north), Bar and Ulcinj (south). Montenegro has twenty-four municipalities.

7. Montenegro is characterized by the uneven economic development of the country – the southern part (the territories of the municipalities of Bar, Budva, Herceg Novi, Kotor, Tivat and Ulcinj), the central part (Cetinje, Danilovgrad, Nikšić and Podgorica) and the northern part (Andrijevica, Berane, Bijelo Polje, Gusinje, Kolašin, Mojkovac, Petnjica, Plav, Pljevlja, Plužine, Rožaje, Šavnik, Žabljak). The northern part accounts for approximately 53% of the territory of Montenegro, while it inhabits only 28.7% of the total population. The northern part is the least developed part of Montenegro, accounting for only 60.2% of the average development in Montenegro in 2015, while the southern region was 69.6% above the average.

8. According to official statistics, the population density in Montenegro is 44.9 persons per square kilometre, and it is one of the lowest in Europe. There is an average of 3.2 persons per household in Montenegro.

9. The major ethnic group is comprised of Montenegrins (45%), followed by Serbs (29%), Bosnians (9%) and Albanians (5%). Orthodox (72%), Islam (19) and Roman Catholicism (3%) are the main religions in Montenegro according to the last census conducted by Statistical Office of Montenegro (in Montenegrin: *Zavod za statistiku Crne Gore*) 2011.

10. In Montenegro, Montenegrin language is in official use. Serbian, Bosnian, Albanian and Croatian languages are also in official use. Cyrillic and Latin alphabets are equal.

11. According to data from official statistics, life expectancy is approximately 76.6 years.

12. Montenegro had always been a pronounced area of emigration. The estimates are that in the period 1953–2006, some 115,000 more people emigrated than immigrated – which is one-third of its natural birth rate. The number of migrants was especially high in the period 1991–2006, which was the result of the breakup of Yugoslavia, the local wars, uncertain livelihood, insecurity and the like. In April 1993, there were 64,258 refugees in Montenegro from the war-torn areas of Croatia and Bosnia-Herzegovina; and during the North Atlantic Treaty Organization intervention of 1999, some 80,000 refugees from Kosovo entered Montenegro.

13. There are no official data on the total number of emigrants since official statistics measure so-called internal migrations. However, it is estimated that more than 600,000 people live outside of Montenegro.

III. Government and Politics

A. *Brief History of Montenegrin Political System*

14. Montenegro, as a country, has a long-standing history. During the eleventh century led by the *Vojislavljević* Dynasty, Montenegro (at the time called: *Duklja*) won its independence from the Byzantine Empire and remained an independent kingdom throughout most of the twelfth century. From the seventeenth century onwards, under the Petrović Dynasty, Montenegrins were struggling for absolute independence from the Ottoman Empire.[2]

15. Modern history of Montenegro starts with the de jure independence which was recognized by the Great Powers at the Congress of Berlin in 1878, following the Montenegrin–Ottoman War. The first Montenegrin Constitution was adopted in 1905, and it had established Montenegro as a parliamentary monarchy under the Petrović Dynasty.

16. During World War I, 1914–1918, Montenegro fought on the side of the Entente forces and had suffered extensive material and human losses. However, at the end of it had lost its statehood.

17. In 1918, it entered the Kingdom of Serbs, Croats, and Slovenians (in Montenegrin: *Kraljevina Srba, Hrvata i Slovenaca*, hereinafter 'KSCS'), in the form of a territorial administrative unit within the KSCS named Banovina of Zeta. In this form, Montenegro existed until 1941. Montenegro was in the period 1918–1941 an agrarian underdeveloped area dominated by a small property, culturally backward, with a high percentage of illiterate population.

18. Within the KSCS, Montenegro was significantly marginalized in political terms, which reflected a lag in other areas of social life.

19. Following World War II and the socialist revolution, Montenegro became one out of six federal units within federal Yugoslavia. On 29 November 1945, the first session of the Constitutional Assembly was held in Belgrade, where the 'Declaration on the proclamation of the Federal People's Republic of Yugoslavia' (in Montenegrin: *Deklaracija o proglašenju Federativne Narodne Republike Jugoslavije*) was adopted. With this decision Yugoslavia ceased to be a monarchy and became a federal republic. The constitution of Yugoslavia since 1963 formally introduced self-management in all areas of the socio-political and economic life of the state. With this constitution, the name of the state was changed to the Socialist Federal Republic of Yugoslavia (hereinafter 'FRY') (in Montenegrin: *Socijalistička federativna republika Jugoslavija*). Under this name, there will be a definitive cessation in 1992.

---

2. Živko Andrijašević, *Istorija Crne Gore* [*History of Montenegro*] 24–202 (2015).

20. In the period after the Second World War, Montenegro, in the framework of the Yugoslav federation, functioned under various names – the People's Republic of Montenegro 1946–1963 (in Montenegrin: *Narodna Republika Crna Gora*), the Socialist Republic of Montenegro 1963–1991 (in Montenegrin: *Socijalistička Republika Crna Gora*) and the Republic of Montenegro since 1992 (in Montenegrin: *Republika Crna Gora*).

21. In federal Yugoslavia, the legislative competence was divided between the federation and the republics. Each republic had its own executive, legislative, and judiciary bodies. The political system in Yugoslavia called 'self-management' (*samoupravljanje*) was different from that of the countries under the Soviet rule. Yugoslavia was not a member of the Warsaw Pact and played a leading role in the Non-Aligned Movement. However, there was one party in power – the Communist Party of Yugoslavia, and the basic postulates of the rule of law did not work in practice. All areas of social, economic and political life were controlled by the ruling party. In the former Yugoslavia, there were no free elections, and basic rights and freedoms, although covered by the Constitution and laws, were only respected if they did not jeopardize the interests of the ruling party.

22. Following the breakup of Yugoslavia, the republics of Serbia and Montenegro together established a federation known as the FRY, which was renamed State Union of Serbia and Montenegro in 2003. Montenegro declared independence on the basis of the independence referendum held in May 2006.

23. In the process of breaking up the Yugoslav federation from six republics, Montenegro did not opt for independence. Montenegro opted for the option of joining Serbia with a federal state. The Montenegrin Parliament issued a referendum with the aim of confirming this commitment by citizens. The referendum was held on 1 March 1992, and 95.94% voted for the option of a state union with Serbia.

24. The constitutional and political development of Montenegro since the breakup of the six-member Yugoslav federation took place in three different stages. The first phase constitutes its constitutional organization as republics-members of the two-member FRY (1992–2002). The creation of the FRY as a two-member federation of Serbia and Montenegro came on 27 April 1992. In the meantime, the international community recognized Slovenia, Croatia and Bosnia and Herzegovina as independent states. The Constitution of the Republic of Montenegro was approved by Montenegro's Parliament on 12 October 1992. It established Montenegro as a democratic ecological and social constituent republic of the FRY, with Serbian as its official language. During the functioning of the common state with Serbia, there was an apparent non-functionality of the created state that resulted from the fact of the great difference in the size, economic and overall strength of Serbia in relation to Montenegro.[3]

---

3. Mijat Šuković, *Three Different Constitutional Arrangements of Montenegro*, 9 J. Const. Theory Phil. L. 43 (2009).

25. The second stage is a constitutional arrangement of Montenegro as a Member State of the atypical State Union of Serbia and Montenegro (2002–2006). Namely, during the federation with Serbia, political disagreements between Montenegro and Serbia were becoming ever more severe, and the question of the need to redefine mutual relations was raised. The organization of the High Representative of the European Union for Common Foreign and Security Policy, on 13 and 14 March 2002, held talks between official representatives of Montenegro and Serbia on the future of relations between Serbia and Montenegro. The result of these negotiations is the document entitled 'The Grounds for Reorganisation of Serbia and Montenegro' (in Montenegrin: *Polazne osnove za preuređenje Srbije i Crne Gore*), signed on 14 March 2002. With this document, was created the state union with the name of Serbia and Montenegro. This ceased to exist in the FRY. The state union bodies were: the Parliament of Serbia and Montenegro, the President of Serbia and Montenegro, who chairs the Council of Ministers, the Court of Serbia and Montenegro, which solves only disputes between the institutions of the state union and between it and its members. In this way, Montenegro has regained the competence to perform all the tasks, except military, diplomatic and consular and flight control.

26. After the referendum on independence which was held, on 21 May 2006, the Parliament of Montenegro adopted the Decision on the proclamation of an independent Montenegro (in Montenegrin: *Odluka o proglašenju nezavisne Crne Gore)*, which establishes its independence with full international legal personality.

27. The third phase constitutes its constitutional organization as an independent state with full international personality (since May 2006). The basic elements of the political-legal order will be described below.

B. Key Features of Political System

28. The current Constitution of Montenegro was ratified and adopted by the Constitutional Parliament of Montenegro on 19 October 2007. The direct cause for the adoption of the Constitution was the declaration of independence of Montenegro in the referendum on independence.

29. The Constitution establishes Montenegro as an independent and sovereign state, with the republican form of government. It also promulgates that Montenegro is a civil, democratic, ecological and the state of social justice, based on the rule of law. Bearer of sovereignty is the citizen with Montenegrin citizenship and exercise power directly and through the freely elected representatives.[4]

30. The political authority in Montenegro is based on and regulated by the Constitution on the principle of the division of powers into the legislative, executive and judicial branch. The legislative power is exercised by the Parliament, the executive power by the Government and the judicial by the courts.

---

4. Constitution of Montenegro (*Ustav Crne Gore, Službeni list Crne Gore* 001/07 and 038/13).

31. The Parliament of Montenegro is the representative body of the citizens. It consists of members of parliament that are elected by citizens in a direct and secret ballot on the basis of a general and equitable voting right. Term of office of the Parliament shall last four years, an MP does not have a binding mandate, they decide and vote according to their own beliefs, and they enjoy immunity and may not be recalled.

32. The Parliament of Montenegro is a legislative body. It adopts Constitution, laws, other regulations and general acts (decisions, conclusions, resolutions, declarations and recommendations). Also, the Parliament confirms international treaties, elect and dismiss from duty the Prime Minister and members of the Government, adopts the budget and performs other duties as transferred to it by the Constitution or the law.[5] Currently, there are eighty-one seats in Montenegrin Parliament.

33. The president of Montenegro represents Montenegro abroad, promulgates laws by ordinance and calls elections for the Parliament of Montenegro. He proposes candidates for Prime Minister of Montenegro to the Parliament. The President of Montenegro is elected on the basis of a general and equal electoral right, through a direct and secret ballot.[6]

34. President also has a role in the legislative process. According to Constitution, the President of Montenegro shall proclaim the law within seven days from the day of adoption of the law, that is, within three days if the law has been adopted under a speedy procedure. Also, the President has a right to send the law back to Parliament for a new decision-making process.[7]

35. Executive power is exercised by the Government of Montenegro. The government is headed by the Prime Minister and consists of the deputy prime ministers and ministers. It manages internal and foreign policy of Montenegro, enforces laws, other regulations and general acts and adopts decrees, decisions and other acts for the enforcement of laws.

36. The exact number of Ministries is not set in Constitution, but is determined by the Government decree tittle: Decree on the organization of work of the state administration (in Montenegrin: *Uredba o organizaciji i načinu rada državne uredbe*) which is often amended.[8] The status of the Agency for Protection of Competition (hereinafter 'Agency'), which will be further analysed in the text below, is governed by this regulation.

5. *Id.*, Art. 82.
6. *Id.*, Art. 95.
7. *Id.*, Art. 94.
8. Decree on the organization of work of the state administration (*Uredba o organizaciji i načinu rada državne uredbe*, *Službeni list Crne Gore* 087/18).

37. Immediately after the declaration of independence and the adoption of the Constitution, Montenegro has identified two strategic foreign and political priorities: membership in the European Union (hereinafter 'EU') and NATO. Montenegro became NATO member on 5 June 2017.

38. On 15 October 2007, Montenegro signed the Stabilisation and Association Agreement (hereinafter 'SAA'). Following ratification by all the EU Member States, the SAA with Montenegro came into force on 1 May 2010. The ratification process took two years and seven months from the date of signing. During this period, the Interim Agreement was in force, regulating trade and trade-related issues that fall under the competences of the European Commission. The SAA's entry into force marked a new phase of integration, which made it formally binding on Montenegro to align its legislation with the EU acquis, as well as to align positions and policies in all areas of cooperation. The quality of SAA's implementation was one of the criteria for receiving the Commission's positive opinion as well as for receiving candidate status, launching negotiations, and the pace of the EU accession process.[9]

39. On 30 November 2009, the EU Council adopted a decision to abolish visas for Montenegro, Macedonia, and Serbia, thus enabling the citizens of these countries to travel without visas to all twenty-five Member States of the Schengen zone – twenty-two EU Member States and four non-EU countries (Iceland, Norway, Switzerland and Liechtenstein). Time has shown that this was a significant day, enabling young people to travel without obstacles and adopt, above all, EU values.

40. On 15 December 2008, Montenegro submitted its application for EU membership. On 22 July, Montenegro received the Questionnaire of the European Commission (in Montenegrin: *Upitnik Evropske komisije*) with questions from all fields of the EU acquis, and that the responses to the Questionnaire represented a basis for the Commission's assessment of Montenegro's readiness to take up commitments arising from the EU membership. On 17 December 2010, the European Council granted Montenegro the status of EU candidate country. In December 2010, Montenegro became a candidate country for EU membership. On 29 June 2012, at the Summit in Brussels, heads of states and governments of the EU confirmed the opening of negotiations on Montenegro's accession to the EU. On 29 June 2012, Montenegro officially began its EU negotiations.

41. A new approach to negotiations was initiated with Montenegro, according to which negotiation chapters 23–Judiciary and fundamental rights and 24–Justice, freedom and security had been opened first, and they would remain open by the end of the negotiation process.[10]

---

9. The information contained in this paragraph derived from internet address: https://www.eu.me/en/montenegro-and-eu/montenegro-eu-relations (last accessed 25 Sep. 2019).
10. The information contained in this paragraph derived from internet address: http://www.skupstina.me/index.php/en/eu-accession/montenegro-and-eu (last accessed 25 Sep. 2019).

42. The competition law issues are found in Chapter 8, entitled – Competition policy. At a bilateral screening in the EU accession process in 2012, Montenegro emphasized that it considered that its antitrust legislation was generally in line with the acquis.[11] In the same report, the European Commission also emphasized that the Law on Protection of Competition of 2012 is generally aligned with the acquis, but also requires further harmonization in certain aspects (e.g., in defining market dominance). At the same time, it is emphasized that it is necessary to further increase the number of employees, budget funds and training, and to ensure complete independence in the decision-making process of the competent agency. Competition law is the subject of constant attention in the European Commission's Annual Progress Reports.

43. Based on the experience gained so far in the accession process, in this chapter the EU requires Montenegro to meet the following conditions: (i) a regulatory framework that is harmonized with the rules on the protection of competition in the EU; (ii) an operationally independent and highly professional body, with sufficient administrative capacity and financial resources, capable of successfully and fully implementing regulations on the protection of competition, and (iii) effective implementation of the regulations in accordance with EU practice, measured, above all, by the number and quality of the decisions made (decisions also confirmed by the competent judicial authorities), and in particular the number and range of the sentences imposed. Unfortunately, apart from the adopted regulations, which are mostly harmonized with the EU law, Montenegro lags significantly behind in meeting the second and third condition.

44. In 2019, Montenegro was the frontrunner in the process of European integration, among the Western Balkans countries. In December 2018, Montenegro opened one more negotiation chapter (Chapter 27 – Environment and climate change). Montenegro now has thirty-two/thirty-three chapters opened and three chapters provisionally closed. The only chapter that is not open is related to the competition policy.

§2. Economic System

45. Within federal Yugoslavia, Montenegro was economically most undeveloped republic. This fact came primarily from the legacy of the earlier organization and state of the economy, but also partly as a consequence of the First and Second World War.

46. Immediately after World War II, in accordance with the current ideology of socialism, state ownership was created. The most important measures by which state property was created were the nationalization of private companies, property confiscation and agrarian reform.

---

11. The information contained in this paragraph derived from internet address: https://www.eu.me/mn/8/item/28 poglavlje-8-konkurencija (last accessed 25 Sep. 2019).

47. The federal Yugoslav economic policy was based on the development of industry in all its years of existence until 1992. The ruling Communist party counted on the revolutionary mass flight after the war, the rich country's raw resources, and the assistance of other socialist countries in this process.

48. The principle of equal development of all the republics of Yugoslavia was to be achieved by accelerated economic development and structural changes throughout the country. Nevertheless, development was to be faster in underdeveloped republics, in order to reach the level of developed republics. In addition, throughout the entire period, Montenegro had a problem of unequal development of its municipalities. Out of twenty municipalities, ten had the treatment of underdeveloped municipalities.

49. The main basis of the Montenegrin industrialization was black metallurgy, steel production (*Željezara Nikšić*) and aluminium (*Kombinat aluminijuma Podgorica*). Additionally, the industry developed in the fields of energy, mechanical engineering and the textile industry.[12]

50. Despite the above facts, until 1989 Montenegrin economy was characterized by very dynamic economic development. The development of the Montenegrin economy in the period 1945–1989 took place on the principles of the development of a socialist self-governing system based on social ownership. Competition in the market of goods and services was not sufficiently developed due to the closure of the domestic economy to the world market and the ruling socialist ideology. The social product in the period 1951–1989 was increased 6.5 times (from USD 218 million to USD 1,400 million).

51. The dynamic economic development of Montenegro from 1952 to 1989 also caused major structural changes in the relation between agriculture and industry. In the realized social product, the industry significantly increased its share from just 7.4% in 1952 to a total of 37.9% in 1989. On the other side, agriculture recorded a reversal trend in the same period because its share of 38.8% fell to 12.6%.

52. The intensive process of industrialization let to dramatic changes in the socio-economic structure of the population. The rapid influx of population in cities and urban areas and their pressure on employment in the secondary and tertiary sector, and above all in the industry, caused high overpopulation and the appearance of technological surpluses, which was especially evident in the 1990s when the process of transition to market economy started.

53. The financial market was reduced to a banking system controlled by the state. Finally, as explained earlier, the political system was under the control of a political party, which led to full domination of politics over the economy.

12. Branislav Marović, *Ekonomska istorija Crne Gore* [*Economic History of Montenegro*] 425–664 (2018).

54. The companies did not go bankrupt despite losses and bad management. In such situations, artificial employment and solution of social problems within the company have a dominant model for solving problems.

55. Along with other countries of the former Yugoslavia, Montenegro has started the transition process in the early nineties of the last century. Unlike the countries of Central and Eastern Europe, many of which have become members of the EU having raised the level of their national competitiveness, Montenegro could not have achieved that for objective reasons, due to international sanctions, wars in the region and broken ties with the former Yugoslav market.

56. The disintegration of the former Yugoslavia broke up the traditional links in trade, exerted a significant effect on the recession and postponed reforms and integration to the EU. Period 1990–1996 is characterized by the economic recession in all areas. The decline in the social product, the rise in unemployment and the decline in employment, the drastic fall in foreign trade, the strengthening of the grey (informal) economy and hyperinflation are the most important features of this period.

57. The suddenness of the changes to the entire political, economic and legal system, the lack of adequately established institutions and the overall system of values inherited from the past, together with the experience of a highly centralized federal state, all significantly hindered the process of implementing significant economic reforms in Montenegro.

58. As of 1997, after the then ruling party underwent certain internal political changes and with substantial aid from international donors, Montenegro began its serious structural transformation in the areas of trade liberalization, privatization, financial sector reform, labour market reform and the reform of the entire business environment. One of the most important areas that required reform was public administration. The main goal of all these activities was to raise the overall level of competitiveness of the economy.

59. The common Yugoslav market functioned with numerous problems in this period. From July 1998, Montenegro officially ceased to pay to the federal budget revenues from customs and part of sales and excise taxes and took over the customs service on its territory. Problems in the functioning of the common Yugoslav market reached a culmination in March 2000, when the trade turnover between Montenegro and Serbia was completely interrupted, which caused the redirection of Montenegro's import-export activities to new markets.

60. In 2001, the Central Bank of Montenegro (in Montenegrin: *Centralna banka Crne Gore*, hereinafter 'CBM') was established. CBM played an important role in the reform of the payment system as well as in the establishment of a stable and efficient payment system. The transition from the dinar to the German mark and then to the euro in 2002 formally confirmed the economic independence of the state and the stability of macroeconomic indicators. After gaining independence in 2006, the period of free economic development began. The average gross domestic product (GDP) growth rate for the period 2006–2018 was around 5%.

61. The reforms started in 1997 began to realize their effects in the period 2001–2007. Reforms conducted have contributed to the macroeconomic stabilization and change of environment for attracting foreign direct investment, which ultimately affected the level of raising national competitiveness. The most important characteristics of this period are the opening up of the economy, the liberalization of foreign flows, the low inflation rate, the budget surplus, the record inflows of foreign direct investments, the continuous reduction of the unemployment rate, the reduction of external debt.

62. In the period from 2001 to 2007, GDP grew about 37% in real terms. In the same period, the net inflow of foreign direct investments was constantly increasing, reaching EUR 678 million in 2007.[13]

63. The process of acceding the EU and NATO had a very strong impact on the economic life of the country. Based on the economic growth and progress, the European Commission has granted Montenegro the official status of a candidate country for EU membership. Montenegro became a member of the World Trade Organization in April 2012, beginning the process of negotiations for membership in the EU the same year.

64. Montenegrin economy, before the outbreak of the global financial and economic crisis, was characterized by rapid growth that was mainly based on the high inflow of foreign direct investment. Based on the structure of the economy from 2006 to 2018, it can be concluded that Montenegrin economy is restructuring towards the economy of services, which was nearly 80% of gross value added at the end of 2018. The most important sectors of industry in Montenegro are energy, tourism, agriculture and trade.

65. The Montenegrin development model considerably changed in the past decade. In the first years after regaining the independence, the economic growth was based on the growth of domestic consumption, caused by the high inflow of foreign direct investment and bank loans. The outbreak of the crisis caused a decline in economic activity, as in most world economies, followed by a hard, but relatively successful recovery period. The economic and financial crisis has revealed a multitude of structural vulnerabilities in the Montenegrin economy. In the period from 2009 to 2012, there was a decline in foreign direct investments, and a negative balance of public finances and rising unemployment.

66. Since 1999, more than 90% of enterprises which were state-owned or majority-owned by the state have been privatized in Montenegro. Nevertheless,

---

13. Nikola Milović & Mijat Jocović, *Impact of Foreign Direct Investment on Competitiveness of Montenegrin Economy*, 16 (1) Transformations Bus. & Econ. 223, 230 (2017).

most of the privatizations have taken place in the sectors of transport, industry, manufacturing, tourism and financial services (banking).

67. Montenegro, as a small and open economy, records a negative balance of trade with foreign countries, with imports significantly exceeding the export. In the structure of exports dominate raw materials and semi-finished products, including base metals, aluminium, food and beverages, and machinery and equipment. The main import products are food, energy, machinery and equipment, mineral products, chemicals and vehicles. The structure of exports is dominated by non-ferrous metals and aluminium, food, electricity and mineral ore.

68. In the twelve-year period after gaining independence (2006–2018), the model of the Montenegrin economy is characterized by an average real growth of 3.2% annually, accompanied by an oscillatory trend of foreign direct investments, an increase in the current account deficit (commodity account), and an increase in public debt. Public finances are weakened by continuous ten-year budget deficits that further affect public debt increases. The financial system is primarily oriented towards a foreign majority-owned banking system that is burdened by a large number of banks in a small economy such as Montenegro, whose gradual consolidation began in 2018.

69. Montenegrin economy recorded the highest growth rates in the two-year period after gaining independence (2006–2008) approximately 7.5% annually, largely based on foreign direct investment inflows and tourism development. Foreign direct investment inflows in 2009 amounted to as much as 41% of GDP (largely driven by the partial privatization of the national generator and distributor of electricity). In the aforementioned period, there was also a high level of borrowing of the economy and population in the banking sector, accompanied by the growth of low quality assets, while both the economy and the population held a net debt position. The resolution of poor quality assets starts in the post-crisis period 2009–2012, while negative economic real growth rates of 5.8% (2009) and 2.7% (2012) were recorded in the same period. With a significant reduction in foreign direct investment and an increase in the current account deficit, starts a gradual increase in public debt of 40% of GDP in 2007, culminating in 2018 with a level of 71% of GDP.

70. The slight recovery of the Montenegrin economy from the global economic crisis began in 2013 when the growth rate was 3.5%. In 2017 and 2018, the economy recorded real growth of 4.7% and 4.9%, respectively, based primarily on major infrastructure projects (construction of the first section of the Bar Boljare highway, infrastructure projects in energy and transport), tourism growth and category of public and private consumption. Viewed through purchasing power parity,

Montenegro's GDP per capita in 2017 was 46% of the EU average, which is an increase of 5% compared to 2008 when it was 41% of the European average.[14]

71. Montenegro's economy is characterized by a double deficit: current account deficit and budget deficit. The main disadvantage of the Montenegrin economy model is reflected in the strong import component. Therefore, the main drivers of the economy over the last two years (investment activity, growth in the number of tourists and higher consumption levels) caused a higher demand for imported goods, bringing the current account deficit in 2018 to 17.2% of GDP or EUR 792.7 million. The negative balance was partly financed by net foreign direct investment (EUR 322.5 million in 2018, or 7% of GDP), while the remainder of deficit financing required additional financial borrowing on the international market through loans (EUR 422.4 million) and securities (EUR 137 million). Historically, the current account deficit has been financed to a large extent through foreign direct investment, that is, portfolio investment, so that in recent years there has been a trend of financing the deficit through the accumulation of Montenegro's external public debt, in which the public sector debt is most characteristic.

72. The budget deficit was recorded for the tenth consecutive year, with the deficit average in the period 2009–2018 was 5% of GDP. In 2018, the budget deficit amounted to EUR 159.2 million (3.5% of GDP) and exceeded the planned amounts. At the end of 2018, public debt stood at 71% of GDP, or EUR 3.27 billion, with Eurobond debt being the largest (seven issuances, out of which those from 2014, 2015, 2016, and 2018 are outstanding). Taking into account the high level of liquidity of the banking sector, a part of the funds for the state budget was also realized through the issuance of bonds on the domestic market. Eurobonds have a maturity of five years, so most of the debt is expected to be repaid in the period 2019–2021, while the repayment of the highway loan will begin in 2021, which will put additional pressure on government finances (loan signed at USD 944 million with Chinese Exim Bank in October 2014 with a repayment period of twenty years and a grace period of six years).

73. Fiscal stabilization is key to further economic development. Since 2017, Montenegro has started implementing the medium-term fiscal consolidation strategy (2017–2020), which is reflected in an increase in the value added tax and excise tax rates, a decrease in wages in the public sector, an improvement in the collection of tax claims, as well as a reduction in certain social allowances, optimization of employment in the public sector. The main objective of fiscal consolidation is to achieve a primary budget surplus in 2019, as well as to reduce public debt below 70% in 2019.[15]

---

14. Financial stability report (published by the Central bank of Montenegro) (available in English): https://www.cbcg.me/en/publications/regular-publications/financial-stability-report (last accessed 11 Oct. 2019).
15. Montenegro Development Directions 2015–2018 (published by the Government of Montenegro) (available in English): http://www.mif.gov.me/en/news/184592/Montenegro-Development-Directions-2018-2021.html (last accessed 11 Oct. 2019).

74. Despite improvements in labour market performance in recent years, the unemployment rate remains high at 15.2%, while the biggest problem is seen in the youth unemployment rate (15–24), which is as high as 30%. Unemployment also shows a high regional disparity, with higher unemployment rates in the northern region compared to the tourist oriented south.

75. Since the introduction of the euro as an official means of payment, price stability in Montenegro has been present with fewer fluctuations in certain years. The inflation rate at the end of 2018 amounted to 1.6%. Montenegro's financial system is dominated by banks (92%), followed by insurance companies (4.6%) and micro-credit financial institutions (1.2%). The banking system is dominated by private ownership, with currently thirteen majority privately owned banks after licences were revoked for two banks in 2018 due to insufficient capitalization. These banks together accounted for around 6% of market share and did not affect the systemic risk sector, thus maintaining stability. The banking system is undoubtedly one of the most important drivers of economic growth with EUR 2.78 billion in net lending activity in 2018, compared to 84 million loans granted in 2001. In addition, there has been a steady increase in the balance sheet sum and deposits, as well as the profitability and efficiency of the overall system.

76. The business environment has not improved significantly in recent years. The biggest shortcomings in terms of investment environment are reflected in the process of starting a new business, electricity supply, property registration and construction permits. From the point of view of the tax system, the Montenegrin economy is attractive for foreign investors. Further improvements are needed in terms of corporate and economic governance, with an emphasis on developing e-governance programmes and strengthening the competition policy framework.

77. The future development of the Montenegrin economy is based on implementing reforms for EU membership, further implementation of the fiscal consolidation strategy and reduction of public debt, investment projects in energy (especially in the part of renewable energy sources), transportation (through airport concession and improvement of road and railway infrastructure), and tourism (development of hotel capacities and tourist facilities), reducing the differences in regional development and further improving the investment climate to attract foreign direct investment.

§3. Legal System

I. General Characteristics of Montenegrin Legal System

78. Montenegro has a relatively long tradition in the regulation of the civil law. The most important act from the legal history of Montenegro is General Code on Property for the Principality of Montenegro (in Montenegrin: *Opšti imovinski zakonik za Knjaževinu Crnu Goru*) emerged in 1888. The author of the Code is widely-known jurist Valtazar Bogišić. The Code represents a codification of property law modelled as per Napoleon's Code Civil. The Code was in force until the 1970s when the former Yugoslavia replaced its previous private law with the Law on Obligations.

79. In the last century, the legal system of Montenegro had to adapt to the different economic and political systems during the transition from socialism to capitalism and subsequently to the harmonization with the EU law in the last decade. Since proclaiming independence, Montenegrin administration has put a lot of effort to build a modern legal system based on the rule of law. However, this process is still at an early stage, and a lot of reforms need to be done in the future period as well.

80. In order to have a clear perception of the Montenegrin legal system in relation to competition law, several facts have to be highlighted.

81. Before proclaiming independence, Montenegrin legal system was part of the ex-Yugoslav legal order, based on ruling socialist ideology. However, important laws passed in Montenegro and ex-Yugoslavia were written to a considerable extent under the influence of developed legal systems of comparative law. In this way, even before the obligations of formal harmonization with EU law, the legal system of Montenegro has set numerous standards of good comparative practice.

82. A significant part of the legislation, especially in terms of the economic system (privatization, banking, trade, foreign investment etc.), has been developed independently by Montenegrin government during federation with Serbia (1992–2006). Finally, in light of the current situation and fulfilment of obligations arising from the SAA, Montenegro must also transpose the EU law in national legal order. Therefore, the current legal system in Montenegro is still, to a certain extent, a mixture of different influences that very often do not have many common characteristics among themselves.

83. At the same time, nowadays, Montenegrin legislation is in a considerable number of areas modern and compatible with the EU law. Generally, the main characteristics of the current situation in drafting and implementing the legislation in Montenegro can be summarized as follows:

(1) Montenegro is achieving a high degree of harmonization of its legal system with the EU law. However, law enforcement institutions do not sufficiently ensure the application of the law in practice. This fact is also evident in the application of competition law in Montenegro. The most significant reasons for this situation are usually the lack of administrative capacity and a non-motivating environment for work in the state administration.
(2) Regulations in many areas are adopted at high speed, which can sometimes lead to problems in monitoring their implementation and raise concerns for mutual harmonization when new laws are passed in related areas. This fact in

competition law will be explained through the relationship between individual sector regulators and the laws governing certain economic sectors and antitrust law.[16]

(3) Due to the need for harmonization with the EU law, national legal tradition and the objective capacity of law enforcement institutions are often neglected. In practice, often important issues that need to be harmonized with the EU law are being introduced ad hoc into existing laws. This creates confusion in the legal system. For example, in competition law, this fact will be described through the relationship between state aid laws and antitrust law.[17]

(4) Sometimes, the passing of the law is not followed by the timely adoption of secondary legislation which limits the quality application of the law.

II. Law-Making Procedure

84. The main sources of law in Montenegro are written laws adopted by the Parliament. The general rule set in Constitution is that laws are adopted by a majority vote of the present Members of the Parliament in the session attended by over one half of the total number of Members. Laws in specific areas require a stricter majority. For example, the Parliament shall decide with a two-thirds majority of votes of all Members on the laws that regulate the electoral system and property rights of foreign citizens.[18]

85. The procedure for passing laws (preparation, proposing, adoption and publication) in Montenegro is regulated by provisions of several legal acts. According to the Constitution, the right to propose laws and other acts is granted to the Government and the Member of the Parliament. The right to propose laws is also granted to six thousand voters, through the Member of the Parliament they authorize.[19]

86. In legislative practice, the legislative initiative is *in the hands* of the Government due to the fact that most laws passed by the Parliament are submitted to adoption by the Government. The organization and manner of work of the Government of Montenegro are more closely regulated by the Rules of Procedure of the Government of Montenegro.[20] In addition to the competent ministry, there is a permanent body within the Government – Commission for Economic Policy and Financial System, which deals with competition law issues. Before formally passing the draft law by the Government and submitting it to the Parliament of Montenegro, a complex procedure is carried out. Specifically, the material for consideration and decision-making at the Government session is submitted in the

16. *See* Part I, Ch. 2, §2 below.
17. *See* Part I, Ch. 3, §4 below.
18. Constitution, Art. 91.
19. *Id.*, Art. 93.
20. Rules of Procedure of the Government of Montenegro (*Poslovnik Vlade Crne Gore, Službeni list Crne Gore* 003/12, 031/15, 048/17, 062/18).

form of a draft law, and afterwards, it is forwarded to the Parliament. In addition to the draft law proposed by the Government to the Parliament, the proposer also submits to the Government a proposal to designate a representative of the Government who will participate in the work of the Parliament and its working bodies.

87. Prior to the consideration at the Government session, along with the draft law, a number of documents with the aim of harmonizing the future law with the legal system of Montenegro, as well as with EU law are submitted. The following documents, *inter alia*, should be submitted: (1) opinion of the Secretariat for Legislation (in Montenegrin: *Sekretarijat za zakonodavstvo*) on the compliance of the draft act with the Constitution and legal system of Montenegro; (2) a statement of compliance of the draft act with the relevant EU regulations, with an accompanying table of compliance; (3) opinion of the Ministry of Justice on the draft act regulating the proceedings before the courts, as well as on the provisions of the draft act regulating sanctions and misdemeanour proceedings; (4) opinion of the Ministry of Public Administration on the proposal of an act regulating the procedure before state bodies, organization of state administration and local self-government; (5) opinion of the Commission for the State Aid Control on the draft act containing certain decisions regarding granting of any type of state aid.[21] All the above documents are provided in the process of drafting the law governing competition.

88. The Rules of Procedure of the Parliament of Montenegro regulates the procedure for passing laws after their proposal.[22] The Parliament sets up committees as their working bodies, which are responsible for reviewing act proposals and performing other tasks within the competence of the Parliament. Issues on the protection of competition are within the competence of the Committee on Economy, Finance and Budget. The Committee works in sessions. Representatives of the proposer of an act and submitters of amendments to the proposal act considered in the sitting take part in the work of the Committee. Representatives of the Government, representatives of scientific and professional institutions, other legal entities and non-governmental organizations, as well as individual professional and scientific workers take part in the work of the Committee if invited, having no right to decide.[23] This is a common practice when system laws are adopted.

89. A law adoption procedure is initiated by submission of a Bill. The Bill is submitted in the form in which the law is adopted, must be reasoned in writing, and delivered in the required number of copies and in electronic form. The President of the Parliament forwards a Bill submitted to the Parliament to MPs and competent Committees, and the same is posted on the website of the Parliament. The President of the Parliament forwards the Bill to the Government unless the Government is its proposer, so it would provide its opinion, within the period which may not exceed

21. *Id.*, Art. 40 para. 1.
22. Rules of Procedure of the Parliament of Montenegro (*Poslovnik o radu Skupštine Crne Gore, Službeni list Republike Crne Gore 051/06, 066/06, 088/09, 080/10, 039/11, 025/12, 049/13, 032/14, 042/15 and 052/17*).
23. *Id.*, Art. 67.

fifteen days from the day of receipt of the Bill. Prior to its consideration in the sitting of the Parliament, a Bill is considered by competent Committees (Legislative Committee and line Committee). The responsible Committee may propose the Parliament to adopt the Bill in whole, adopt it in the wording amended in relation to the wording submitted by the proposer or not adopt the Bill.[24]

90. Finally, the Law on Publication of Regulations and Other Acts provides that laws and other regulations passed by the competent authorities of Montenegro shall be published in the 'Official Gazette of Montenegro'.[25] The Law stipulates that in addition to the Constitution and laws, the Official Gazette shall, *inter alia,* also publish: decrees, decisions and other acts of the Government; by-laws and other acts passed by ministries; decisions and other acts of the Constitutional Court of Montenegro; acts of the Judicial Council, judicial bodies, the Prosecutorial Council and the State Prosecutor's Office, as provided by law; judgments of the European Court of Human Rights relating to Montenegro; acts of regulatory bodies, other legal entities and persons (councils, commissions, etc.) enacted in the exercise of public authority; regulations of municipal authorities.[26] Publication of laws, other regulations and acts in the Official Gazette of Montenegro is an activity of public interest.

III. Courts System in Montenegro

91. In the application of competition law in practice, courts have a special role. The process of reforming the judicial system is one of the most important processes in the last decade in Montenegro. In the previous period, a number of positive developments in the field of judicial reform have been made: clarification of preconditions for strengthening the independence of the judiciary, improving the transparency of the work of the courts, reducing the number of backlog cases, establishing a judicial information system (hereinafter 'JIS'), etc. Efficiency and accountability of the judiciary are the main challenges in the development of the judicial system in Montenegro.

92. The principle of independence of the judiciary is proclaimed by the Constitution of Montenegro, laws and international treaties. The Constitution proclaimed the principle of the division of power into legislative, executive and judicial power. The relationship of power rests on balance and mutual control. Judicial power is exercised by courts whose organization and functioning are based on the constitutionally guaranteed principle of independence and autonomy. Judicial function is permanent. Judges enjoy functional immunity, and they can be dismissed and serve their judicial function only in cases prescribed by the Constitution.[27]

---

24. *Id.*, Art. 138.
25. Law on Publication of Regulations and Other Acts (*Zakon o objavljivanju propisa i drugih akata, Službeni list Crne Gore* 005/08).
26. *Id.*, Art. 5 para. 1.
27. Constitution, Art. 121.

93. In Montenegro, Law on Courts regulates establishment, organization and jurisdiction of the courts, requirements for the election of judges and lay judges, organization of the work in courts, judicial administration, financing of the courts and other issues relevant to orderly and timely functioning of the courts.[28]

94. Courts are organized in a single, integral way with a simplified organization based on three layers of adjudication. An important advantage of such a system is its efficiency. In Montenegro, there are courts of general jurisdiction and the specialized courts. The courts of general jurisdiction are: misdemeanour courts, basic courts, high courts, the Court of Appeal, and the Supreme Court. The specialized courts are: the Commercial Court and the Administrative Court.[29]

95. There are three misdemeanour courts for the whole territory of Montenegro (in Bijelo Polje, Budva and Podgorica) and are deciding over misdemeanour offences. The High Misdemeanour Court decides over appeals to the decisions of the mentioned misdemeanour courts. The role of the misdemeanour courts in relation to the competition law will be deeper elaborate in further text.[30]

96. Montenegro has fifteen basic courts with jurisdiction in criminal, civil, labour cases and other legal matters. There are two high courts with the seats in Bijelo Polje and Podgorica. The high courts have a jurisdiction to decide in the first instance over specific criminal cases. Also, the high courts have a jurisdiction to decide in the second instance over appeals against decisions of basic courts both in criminal and civil cases.[31]

97. There is a single commercial court for the whole territory of Montenegro. It has jurisdiction *inter alia* over disputes relating to the distortion of competition, abuse of monopolistic or dominant position on the market and entering into monopolistic agreements.[32] The Court of Appeal decides over appeals to the high court's decisions in the first instance as well as on appeals to the decisions of the Commercial Court and resolves conflicts of jurisdictions between basic courts from the territories of the high courts, basic courts and the high courts, and between the high courts.[33]

98. The Administrative Court has its seat in Podgorica and decides over administrative cases. The Administrative Court has an important role in applying competition law in practice, which will be highlighted in detail in further text.[34]

---

28. Law on Courts (*Zakon o sudovima, Službeni list Crne Gore* 011/15).
29. Mladen Vukčević & Miloš Bošković, *Judicial System in Montenegro: Historical Development, Basic Principles, and Organisation*, 13 L. & Just. Rev. 26 (2016).
30. *See* Part I, Ch. 5, §1, IV below.
31. Law on Courts, Art. 16.
32. *Id.*, Art. 18.
33. *Id.*, Art. 20.
34. *See* Part III, Ch. 4, §1 below.

99. The highest court in Montenegro is the Supreme Court. The Supreme Court takes general legal standpoints on disputable legal matters arising from case law, in view of ensuring uniformity in the application of the law by the courts. The general legal standpoint may be taken ex officio or at the request of a court. In accordance with the Constitution, the Supreme Court shall secure unified enforcement of laws by the courts.[35]

100. According to the European Commission progress report for 2018, the rule of law is among the biggest challenges for Montenegro in the future period.[36]

101. The Judicial Councils of Montenegro is the key body in charge of managing the judicial system and the careers of judges. Judicial Council of Montenegro was established by the Constitution of Montenegro and the Law on Judicial Council and Judges as an independent and autonomous body that ensures and guarantees the independence, autonomy, responsibility and professionalism of the courts and judges.[37] Its composition and appointment procedures are broadly in line with European standards.

102. The members of the Council, by their position, are the President of the Supreme Court and the Minister in charge of the judiciary. Eight elective members of the Council consist of four judges and four members from the rank of eminent legal professionals with at least fifteen years of experience in the profession and who enjoy a personal and professional reputation.

103. The Judicial Council has significant powers that relate primarily to the election of judges and control of their work. In accordance with the constitutional and legal competences, the Council *inter alia*: (1) elects and dismisses from office the President of the Supreme Court, (2) elects and dismisses from office the President of the Judicial Council, (3) submits to the Parliament an annual report on the work of the Judicial Council and the overall situation in the judiciary, (4) elects and dismisses from office a judge, a president of a court and a lay judge, (5) deliberates on the work report of a court, applications and complaints regarding the work of the court and take positions thereon, (6) determines termination of judicial office, (7) determines the number of judges and lay judges, (8) decides on the disciplinary responsibility of judges and court presidents, (9) provides the use, functionality and uniformity of the JIS in part related to courts, (10) considers complaints on the work of judges and court presidents, (11) deliberates on complaints of judges and takes positions regarding threats to their independence and autonomy, (12) elects the disciplinary prosecutor, (13) gives opinions on draft regulations in the field of judiciary and performs other tasks stipulated by law.

---

35. Constitution of Montenegro, Art. 124 para. 2.
36. EC progress report for 2018, available at: https://ec.europa.eu/neighbourhood-enlargement/sites/near/files/20180417-montenegro-report.pdf (last accessed 25 Sep. 2019).
37. Law on Judicial Council and Judges (*Zakon o sudskom savjetu i sudijama, Službeni list Crne Gore* 11/2015, 28/2015, 42/18).

104. According to the European Commission progress report for 2018, constitutional and legal guarantees ensuring judicial independence are in place, but the judiciary is still perceived as vulnerable to political interference.

105. The Law on Courts guarantees the principle of random allocation of cases. The establishment of the system of random allocation of cases began in 2002, but it was only put into practice in 2013 by the introduction of the JIS. JIS enables electronic recording of data about the subject, as well as a random selection of a judge, through set electronic parameters and algorithms, without the influence of a human factor. The European Commission, in its progress reports since 2011, highlighted that in practice, random allocation of cases is implemented automatically through JIS, although for very small courts there are certain limits in this regard. Also, JIS has not been introduced in misdemeanour courts.[38]

106. According to the Annual Report of the Judicial Council for 2018, 144 complaints were filed to the Judicial Council, 9 complaints more than in 2017, 6.25% respectively. After reviewing the complaints at the sessions of the Judicial Council, it took a position in 87 cases, while for the remaining 57 complaints, the proceedings are still in progress. The complaints were mainly related to the dissatisfaction of the parties with the manner of conducting the proceedings, the content of procedural decisions made during the proceedings, with the first and second instance decisions, as well as decisions on extraordinary legal remedies which were made at their expense. One part of the complaints relates to the long duration of the proceedings.[39]

107. The Constitution of Montenegro prescribes that everyone has the right to fair and public trial within a reasonable time before an independent, impartial court established by the law. Protection of the right to a trial within a reasonable time, as well as just satisfaction due to a violation of the right to a trial within a reasonable time, is exercised in court proceedings, in the manner and under the conditions prescribed by the Law on Protection of the Right to Trial Within a Reasonable Time.[40] The legal remedies for the protection of the right to a trial within a reasonable time are the requests to expedite the proceedings (in Montenegrin: *zahtjev za ubrzanje postupka*) and the claim for just satisfaction (in Montenegrin: *tužba za pravično zadovoljenje*). In 2018, there were a total of 354 pending control requests, 344 were resolved, while 10 remained unresolved.[41] Finally, after terminated proceedings, the initiated claims for just satisfaction, in which the violation of the right to trial within

38. Pravo na nezavisan i nepristrasan sud slučajna dodjela predmeta u sudovima u Crnoj Gori (published by the Human rights action), available at (in Montenegrin): http://www.hraction.org/wp-content/uploads/Slucajna_raspodjela_18_nov_2014.pdf (last accessed 25 Sep. 2019).
39. Annual report on the work of the Judicial Council and total balance in the judiciary for 2018, available at (in Montenegrin): https://sudovi.me/podaci/sscg/dokumenta/10967.pdf (last accessed 25 Sep. 2019).
40. Law on Protection of the Right to Trial Within a Reasonable Time (*Zakon o zaštiti prava na suđenje u razumnom roku, Službeni list Crne Gore* 011/07).
41. Annual Report of the Judicial Council for 2018, p. 35.

a reasonable time was determined, at the non-pecuniary damage was awarded a total of EUR 42,700, which is considerably higher compared to 2016, when at the same basis, was awarded EUR 24,000.

108. According to the official judicial statistics, there are 257 employed judges in Montenegro. About 60% of this number are women. Montenegrin courts started 2018 with 40,781 cases, received 98,786 – resolved 97,696 cases, while 38,971 cases (28.52%) remained unresolved. The inflow of cases was lower compared to 2017 by 2.81%, and the number of resolved cases was higher by 6.89% compared to the previous year. The average monthly influx per judge was 33.33 cases, 395.53 were resolved and 157.78 unresolved cases remained per judge, annually.

109. Case law of Montenegrin courts is an important interpretative instrument but is officially not a binding source of law. In the process of EU accession, judicial practice is gaining an increasingly important role. First, the Court of Justice of the European Union (hereinafter 'CJEU') case law is an important source of EU law. Second, many institutions in Montenegro, among them the Agency, in their work and interpretation of national law, rely on the judgments of the CJEU.

110. Since 2011, the web portal of courts has been officially launched. It contains websites of all courts, as well as the Judicial Council website.[42] Court decisions are available on a special portal. Extracts from the decisions of the European Court of Human Rights are published on the Supreme Court website. The training of judges is continually implemented in the field of monitoring and implementation of the European Court of Human Rights practice. In courts with more departments, councils or departments of court practice have been established. This contributes to the harmonization of domestic jurisprudence. Nevertheless, it is necessary to continue to familiarize judges with the practice of the CJEU, primarily because of the fact that the date of Montenegro's membership in the EU, the case law will become an integral part of the Montenegrin legal system.

111. There is, unfortunately, no detailed official statistics available that would enable to detect only competition law related cases.

§4. Historical Background of Antitrust Law

112. Origin of the competition law on the territory of Montenegro can be found back to 1930. Namely, the Kingdom of Yugoslavia adopted Law on Suppression on Unfair Competition 1930 (in Montenegrin: *Zakon o suzbijanju nelojalne konkurencije*) and Decree on Cartels 1935 (in Montenegrin: *Uredba o kartelima*). In accordance with this act, cartels were not prohibited per se, but they were under the control of the state. Also, the institutional framework for monitoring cartels was established within the jurisdiction of the Ministry for Trade and Industry.

42. Available at (in Montenegrin): www.sudovi.me (last accessed 25 Sep. 2019).

113. As elaborated in the earlier chapter about the economic system, the centralized economy did not make room for free market and competition. Despite this fact, ex-Yugoslavia adopted some pieces of legislation which contained elements of competition. For example, the element of competition law can be found in Law on Regulation of Business Relation on the market from 1962[43] and Law on Suppression on Unfair Competition and Monopoly Agreements from 1974.[44] Finally, general norms in relation to this matter can be found in the Law on Obligations from 1978.[45] According to this legislation, unfair competition, monopolistic agreements and abuse of dominant position were prohibited. For example, in accordance with Article 3 of the Law on Suppression on Unfair Competition and Monopoly Agreements from 1974, monopolistic agreements were *agreements of two or more Basic Organization of Associated Labour on trade conditions with a purpose to restrict or prevent free competition and enable one or more organizations to achieve a monopolistic or otherwise privileged position with regard to other organization or consumers.*

114. Law on Trade from 1990 was the last attempt of the legislators to regulate the competition law within the socialist legal system.[46] For the first time, this law envisaged a special body in charge of monitoring and applying the monopolistic operations – Commission for protection against monopolistic activity (in Montenegrin: *Komisija za zaštitu od monopolističkog djelovanja).*[47] All these acts were more symbolic expressions of the intention of the dominant ideology of socialism in order to distinguish from communism and to express the new face of economic ideology. Of course, implementation of these legal acts was limited due to overall legal, economic and political circumstances.

115. Montenegro has a short tradition in independent regulation of the competition law.

116. Legal framework of competition law in Montenegro in the last twenty years can be divided into several periods.[48]

117. The period 1996–2006, during the FRY, after the State Union of Serbia and Montenegro. This period is characterized by the application of Antimonopoly Law of Yugoslavia, on the basis of which we can conclude that Montenegro did not have a system of competition law.[49] In addition, federal authority, the Antimonopoly

---

43. Law on Regulation of Business Relation on the market from 1962 (*Zakon o regulisanju poslovnih odnosa na tržištu, Službeni list FNRJ* 030/62).
44. Law on Suppression on Unlawful Competition and Monopoly Agreements (*Zakon o suzbijanju nelojalne utakmice i monopolističkih sporazuma, Službeni list SFRJ* 24/74).
45. Law on Obligations (*Zakon o obligacionim odnosima, Službeni list SFRJ* 29/78).
46. Law on Trade (*Zakon o trgovini, Službeni list SFRJ* 046/90).
47. *See* Ivan Đekić, *Politika zaštite konkurencije u Srbiji – stanje i perspektive* [*Competition Policy in Serbia: State and Perspectives*], Ekonomske teme 229, 240 (2009).
48. *See* Andrea Marušić & Nikola Milović, *Competition Policy in Montenegro,* 111–128 (Slavica Penev ed., Westminster Foundation for Democracy 2013).
49. Antimonopoly Law (*Antimonopolski zakon, Službeni list SRJ* 29/1996).

Commission was responsible for the implementation of this law. The staff, organization and jurisdiction of this Commission were taken over by the Republic of Serbia, while Montenegro did not have established specialized body responsible for the implementation of this law. Also, the Montenegrin judicial practice, until the new law was adopted in 2006, did not record any case run due to the impairments in this field.

118. Period 2006–2012, when the implementation of the competition rules was regulated by the Law on Protection of Competition of the Republic of Montenegro (hereinafter '2006 Competition Act'),[50] which entered into force on 1 January 2006, and it was valid until the new Law on Protection of Competition was adopted in 2012. By adopting the 2006 Competition Act, Montenegro for the first time as an independent country prohibited cartels and abuse of dominant position.

119. The actual period from 2012, which is characterized by adoption and implementation of the new Law on Protection of Competition of Montenegro (hereinafter 'Competition Act'),[51] entered into force on 8 October 2012. In 2012, by adopting the Competition Act, Montenegro started a new, very demanding phase of development of competition law which is striving to be harmonized with EU legislation. Elements of the new Competition Act will be elaborated further in the text.

120. The 2006 Competition Act is the first adopted law in this area in Montenegro, which establishes and regulates basic principles of competition law and the institutional framework for their implementation. The law was largely compliant with the EU law, competition law standards set forth in sections 101, 102 and 106 of the Treaty on the Functioning of the European Union (hereinafter 'TFEU'), as well as with the key EU regulations and directives in this field. The first amendment of this Law was adopted in May 2007.[52]

121. In accordance with the 2006 Competition Act in order to secure its full implementation, several by-laws have been adopted. The most important by-laws adopted on the basis of the 2006 Competition Act relate to the following:

- Decree on detailed conditions for the exemption by species and determining the types of agreements that may be exempted from the law.[53]
- Rulebook on the content of the request for individual exemptions.[54]
- Rulebook on the content of the application of agreement and manner of keeping the record.[55]

50. Law on Protection of Competition (*Zakon o zaštiti konkurencije, Službeni list Crne Gore* 69/05).
51. Law on Protection of Competition (*Zakon o zaštiti konkurencije, Službeni list Crne Gore* 44/2012).
52. Law on Amendments to the Law on Protection of Competition (*Zakon o izmjenama i dopunama Zakona o zaštiti konkurencije, Službeni list Crne Gore* 37/07).
53. *Uredba o bližim uslovima za izuzeća sporazuma po vrstama i određivanje vrsta sporazuma koji mogu biti izuzeti od zakona, Službeni list Crne Gore* 10/07.
54. *Pravilnik o sadržaju zahtjeva za pojedinačna izuzeća, Službeni list Crne Gore* 36/06.
55. *Pravilnik o sadržini prijave sporazuma i načinu vođenja evidencije, Službeni list Crne Gore* 54/06.

- Rulebook on form and content of the application for registration of approved concentrations and form of register and manner of keeping it.[56]
- Rulebook on form and content of the request for procedure initiating.[57]
- Instruction on form and content of the request for issuance of approval for concentration application.[58]
- Instruction on criteria for determining the relevant market.[59]

122. Experience and practical application of the 2006 Competition Act emphasized the following weaknesses and lack of the legislation:

(1) Practice in the implementation of the law has shown that the threshold of annual income was set too low. It was necessary to set a higher threshold of annual income to take into consideration a significant concentration, which would have a major impact on competition. Also, this lack influenced the inability of responsible institutions to focus on cartels and abuses of dominant position.
(2) It was a short deadline for submitting the request for issuing approval for concentration.
(3) Penalty provisions were significantly disabled and hampered actions against the perpetrator.
(4) There was no defined obligation to inform the party in the procedure before passing the decision on impairments of competition.
(5) Lack of special authorization of the Agency (Leniency programme).[60]

123. First competition authority in Montenegro was established as a Department for Protection of Competition as part of the Ministry of Economy in 2006, lacking independence in its work and transparency. This Department was transformed in the Directorate for Protection of Competition, as a body within the Ministry of Economy in 2008. An independent competition authority was finally established in 2012, based on the new Competition Act.

124. By the 2006 Competition Act, there were certain powers on the side of the Ministry of Economy and to the Directorate for Protection of Competition. Therefore, there was no independent institution responsible for the overall implementation of competition policy. For example, the Ministry was, *inter alia*, authorized to propose a policy of protection and development of competition, monitor implementation of the competition protection and development policy; to pass regulations for the implementation of this law, etc. On the other hand, the Competition protection directorate was in charge of submitting decisions in the procedure for determining

56. *Pravilnik o obliku i sadržini prijave za registraciju odobrenih koncentracija i obrascu registra i načinu vođenja, Službeni list Crne Gore* 36/06.
57. *Pravilnik o obliku i sadržini zahtjeva za pokretanje postupka, Službeni list Crne Gore* 36/06.
58. *Uputstvo o obliku i sadržini zahtjeva za izdavanje odobrenja za sprovođenje koncentracije, Službeni list Republike Crne Gore* 77/05.
59. *Uputstvo o kriterijima za utvrđivanje relevantnog tržišta, Službeni list Republike Crne Gore* 77/05.
60. *See* Nikola Milović, *Competitiveness and Institutional Framework for Implementation of Competition Policy in Montenegro,* Economic themes 641, 654 (2010).

the violation of competition and granting exemptions from the prohibition of individual agreements and approve the concentration.

125. In order to understand the limited role that the Directorate for Competition has undoubtedly played, it is also necessary to point out the circumstances in which it operated. First, it was formed immediately after the declaration of independence in a time of accelerated economic growth of a country in which the issue of protection of competition law was not among the political priorities of the then Government. Second, during the period of its functioning, there were no open negotiations on EU membership, so the specific results in antitrust policy have not been taken into account sufficiently. The functioning of this body was characterized by the following (limiting) factors:

(1) Insufficient number of qualified staff.
(2) Lack of financial resources for the functioning of the Directorate.
(3) Lack of transparency (e.g., annual reports were not available to the public).
(4) Insufficient level of independence, with too narrow and insufficient authorization.
(5) Lack of power to impose sanctions on undertakings that violated competition law.[61]

126. In the framework of the mentioned legislation and institutional framework, in June 2008, the Ministry of Economy drafted the Strategy of Competition Policy that has defined the situation in the field of competition, objectives, priorities, and means to achieve them, as well as the necessary resources for the effective implementation of the competition rules.[62] The ultimate goal of this strategy was to complete the harmonization of competition and legal provisions with European provisions as well as the effective implementation of policies through independent functionality of the competent authorities. The strategy presented a basis for future phases of the development of competition policy in Montenegro, especially in the field of analysis of progress in the application of competition rules and the establishment of professional and independent institutions. The Strategy was aimed to provide the Competition Act to be harmonized with the EU legal framework in the field of competition.

127. Despite the fact that the 2006 Competition Act had its positive effects, its implementation effects were weak due to the limited power of established institution for the protection of competition as well as lack of human resources for implementation. Finally, the lack of political will to have stronger initiation was visible in the first year of implementation of this Law. However, things start to change after signing SAA, mostly due to the fact that Montenegro obliged to harmonize its legislation with the EU.

61. *Id.*
62. Strategy of the Competition Policy (published by the Government of Montenegro, Ministry for Economic Development), available (in Montenegrin): http://www.minekon.gov.me/files/1234792267.pdf (last accessed 5 Jul. 2019).

128. The period from 2012 to the present can be viewed in different ways. Undoubtedly, the capacities of the competent state authority for the protection of competition have been significantly improved in the past period. However, the public is under the impression that cases of impairment of competition law are not sufficiently processed, and overall confidence in the work of the institution is low. The most significant argument for this position is that there is a total low number of procedures with a final judgment in the area of cartel agreements and abuse of a dominant position.

129. Thus, for the time being, a sufficient number of cases have not been created in the practice of the Agency, on the basis of which an argumentative position on the quality of the application of the law in this field can be taken. There are several reasons for this situation – a misunderstanding of the importance and role of competition law, the insufficient administrative capacity of the agency, and the like.

130. However, many of the reasons for this situation, as will be explained below, are not on the Agency's side, but are the result of the systemic situation in the country's legal system. First, the legal system in which the Agency operates is complex. In practice, two proceedings are being conducted against its decisions before two different courts – an administrative dispute before an Administrative Court and a misdemeanour procedure before a competent Misdemeanour Court. In proceedings before the Administrative Court, which most often seeks to annul the Agency's decision by the Administrative Court, as explained below, no substantive provisions are taken into account in practice, but the Agency's decisions are annulled because of omissions in conducting the proceedings. Second, the application of the provisions of the administrative procedure before the Agency in the process of establishing impairment of competition leads to meaningless situations that objectively prevent the Agency from conducting the proceedings for establishing the impairment of competition law in a qualitative and effective manner. Due to the aforementioned, the proceedings are lengthy, as the parties to the proceedings significantly abuse their procedural powers. Third, the Agency is not authorized to impose a misdemeanour but initiates misdemeanour proceedings before a competent Misdemeanour Court. Proceedings before these courts take a long time in practice, and there are often cases for establishing the impairment of competition conducted by the Agency which do not result in misdemeanour sanctions for the perpetrator, for formal reasons (statute of limitations, discharge, etc.).

131. Lastly, one of the indicators of a lack of awareness of competition law is the fact that a negligible number of compensation cases are initiated by private entities. Also, there are no cases where criminal liability for violation of the competition law provisions has been established. All of the above also affected the scope and quality of the work of this monograph, as without analysing a significant number of individual cases, it is not possible to take general positions on the quality of application of certain competition law principles in practice.

Part I. Structure of Antitrust Law and Its Enforcement

Chapter 1. Sources of Antitrust Law

§1. National Sources

132. Elements of antitrust regulation could be found in various legal sources with different legal nature (constitution, laws and by-law legislation).

133. According to the Constitution, the economic system of Montenegro is based on a free and open market, freedom of entrepreneurship and competition, independence of the economic entities and their responsibility for the obligations accepted in the legal undertakings, protection and equality of all forms of property.[63] Constitution prohibits acts which obstruct and limit free competition and encourage unequal, monopolistic or dominant position in the market.[64] These norms in practice do not have a significant effect for enforcement of antitrust regulation but are often used by parties and courts in the reasoning of a lawsuit or a judgment.

134. The Competition Act is the basic source of competition law in Montenegro. The content of the Competition Act is mostly harmonized with EU competition law and its main substantive provisions originating from the TFEU. In addition, the basic principles of the protection of competition are also contained in the provisions of legislation governing particular sectors such as telecommunications, banking, insurance, energy, media, etc.

135. Finally, national sources of competition law are contained in sub-law legislation adopted by the Government, line ministries and by the Agency.

136. The Constitution of Montenegro has clearly established the boundary between laws and by-laws, prescribing issues that can only be regulated by law. In accordance with the Constitution, the law shall regulate:

(1) the manner of exercise of human rights and liberties, when this is necessary for their exercise;

---

63. Constitution, Art. 139 para. 1.
64. *Id.*, Art. 139 para. 2.

(2) the manner of exercise of the special minority rights;
(3) the manner of establishment, organization and competences of the authorities and the procedure before those authorities if so required for their operation;
(4) the system of local self-government;
(5) other matters of interest for Montenegro.[65]

137. By means of by-laws, it is possible, in order to implement the law, to elaborate in detail the issues that are regulated by law. Authorization for the adoption of a by-law and issues that can be regulated by a by-law must be prescribed by law.[66] In the last years, in the legal system of Montenegro, there is a practice that a significant number of issues that are subject of the law are regulated by by-laws.

138. In accordance with the Constitution of Montenegro, any person may file an initiative to start the procedure for the assessment of constitutionality and legality. The procedure before the Constitutional Court for the assessment of constitutionality and legality may be initiated by the court, other state authority, local self-government authority and five Members of the Parliament.[67] During the procedure, the Constitutional court may order to stop the enforcement of an individual act or actions that have been taken on the basis of the law, other regulation or general act, the legality of which is being assessed if the enforcement thereof could cause irreparable damage. In the matter of competition law, there were no cases brought before the Constitutional court for the assessment of the legality of the adopted by-laws.

§2. International Sources

139. The Constitution of Montenegro regulates the issue of legal power and place of the international agreements in the legal system. In accordance with the Constitution, the ratified and published international agreements and generally accepted rules of international law are an integral part of the internal legal order. They have the supremacy over the national legislation and apply directly when they regulate relations differently than the national legislation.[68] The Montenegrin Constitution has accepted a monistic understanding of the relationship between international and internal law, according to which international and internal law is part of a system in which there is a hierarchy. The norm of national law cannot derogate from the norms of international law under any circumstances. The primacy of international law has determined the content of the principles of constitutionality and legality that establish the hierarchy of legal acts. Thus, the law must be in conformity with the Constitution and confirmed and published international agreements, and if it not, the Constitutional court may eliminate it from the legal system by its

65. *Id.*, Art. 16.
66. Dušanka Jauković & Slavica Bajić, *Ustavni sistem Crne Gore* [*Constitutional System of Montenegro*] 12–73 (2015).
67. Constitution, Art. 150.
68. *Id.*, Art. 9.

decision. The Constitution stipulates that international agreements are concluded by the Government of Montenegro[69] and confirmed by the Parliament of Montenegro.[70]

140. The Constitutional Law on Implementation of the Constitution of Montenegro of 2007 stipulated the obligation to comply with the new Constitution with all the legislation in the period of two years from its adoption.[71] One of the envisaged obligations was the adoption of a special law, in order to regulate the matter of the conclusion and confirmation of international treaties in an independent Montenegro. The Law on Conclusion and Execution of International Treaties of 2008 regulates the procedure for the conclusion, confirmation and enforcement of international treaties.[72] In accordance with this Law, the Parliament of Montenegro confirms (1) international agreements that require the issuance of new or amendments to the applicable laws; (2) international treaties concerning the accession to political or military alliances; (3) international treaties whose provisions explicitly provide for their confirmation.[73] The international agreement is confirmed by law. The Law on Confirmation of International Treaties has to be published in the 'Official Gazette of Montenegro – International Treaties' before its entry into force under international law.

141. Most important international source of competition law in Montenegro is SAA with the EU. Since signing SAA, it was not enough to have laws compatible with EU *acquis*, Montenegro also needs to secure its enforcement in practice. In accordance with the SAA, Montenegro shall endeavour to ensure that its existing laws and future legislation will be gradually made compatible with the Community *acquis*. Also, Montenegro shall ensure that existing and future legislation will be properly implemented and enforced.

142. The SAA contains substantive competition law provisions in Article 73.1 (i) and (ii), and they read as follows:

> The following are incompatible with the proper functioning of this Agreement, insofar as they may affect trade between the Community and Montenegro:
>
> (i) all Agreements between undertakings, decisions by associations of undertakings and concerted practices between undertakings which have as their object or effect the prevention, restriction or distortion of competition;

69. *Id.*, Art. 100 para. 4.
70. *Id.*, Art. 82 para. 17.
71. The Constitutional Law on the Implementation of the Constitution of Montenegro (*Ustavni Zakon za sprovođenje ustava Crne Gore, Službeni list Crne Gore* 001/07, 009/08, 004/09, 071/09, 022/10, 080/10, 027/11 and 038/11).
72. The Law on the conclusion and execution of international treaties (*Zakon o zaključenju i izvršenju međunarodnih ugovora, Službeni list Crne Gore* 077/08).
73. *Id.*, Art. 14.

(ii) abuse by one or more undertakings of a dominant position in the territories of the Community or Montenegro as a whole or in a substantial part thereof.

143. In addition, in accordance with Article 73.2 of the SAA:

> Any practices contrary to this article shall be assessed on the basis of criteria arising from the application of the competition rules applicable in the Community, in particular, from Articles 81, 82, 86 and 87 of the EC Treaty and interpretative instruments adopted by the Community institutions.

144. Montenegro undertakes an obligation to establish an operationally independent authority which is entrusted with the powers necessary for the full application of Article 73.1 (i) and (ii).

145. Taking into account the above-mentioned provision, the Montenegrin Agency for Competition is obliged to appropriately apply, the criteria arising from the application of the rules on the protection of competition in EU. In practice, the Agency applies the primary Montenegrin regulations, and in the case of legal gaps or dilemmas in the interpretation, it applies the criteria from the EU competition law, which includes the regulations and guidelines of the EU, as well as the decisions of the European Commission, the decisions of the European Courts and other institutions of the EU.

146. The EC, when assessing progress in the implementation of the SAA, paid special attention to this area since it was determined in the Agreement as one of the priorities for harmonization.

§3. Secondary Sources

I. Regulations

147. In addition to the Constitution and the special law regulating the matter of competition, this issue is regulated in Montenegro by the by-laws of the Government. In the field of competition law, a number of decrees (in Montenegrin: *Uredba*) were adopted by the Government, while line ministries were responsible for the adoption of other by-laws (rulebooks and guidance, in Montenegrin: *pravilnici i uputstva*). In general, the Government adopts decrees, decisions and other acts for the enforcement of laws. During the state of war or the state of emergency, the Government may adopt decrees with the power of the law if the Parliament is not able to meet.[74]

74. Constitution, Art. 101 para. 1.

148. In Montenegrin legal system, a decree is a legal act of the Government and in the hierarchy of legal regulations is the highest by-law after the law. The decree has to be published in the Official Gazette of Montenegro and shall enter into force no later than the eighth day after the date of their publication. Exceptionally, when there are reasons for this in the adoption procedure, the regulation may enter into force at the earliest date of publication.

149. Ministries adopt rulebooks, orders and guidance. The common characteristic of these acts is that they cannot establish rights and obligations for individuals and legal entities. A rulebook is an act that elaborates in more detail certain provisions of laws and other regulations. Ministries adopt rulebooks when they are authorized by law and are always within the boundaries of the powers contained in that law. Order is an act of a ministry ordering or prohibiting conduct in a particular situation of a general nature. The orders have not been passed in the field of competition law so far. The guidance is a legal act that prescribes the manner of work and performance of the affairs of the administrative body.

150. The Competition Act provides the legal basis for the adoption of more detailed regulations by the Government of Montenegro. In accordance with Article 11 of the Competition Act, the Government may specify conditions, procedure and criteria for group exemptions by categories of agreements. The Competition Act set the main content of this act, and they are as follows:

(1) categories of agreements that may be exempted;
(2) restrictions and conditions that the categories of agreements may not contain;
(3) other conditions that the parties to the agreement must fulfil and with which the agreements must comply and, in particular, the periods of validity of agreements and exemptions.[75]

151. On this basis, the Government has so far adopted several block exemption decrees:

- Decree on group exemption of vertical agreements (hereinafter 'Vertical BED').[76]
- Decree on group exemption of horizontal research and development agreements (hereinafter 'R&D BED').[77]
- Decree on group exemption of horizontal specialization agreements (hereinafter 'Specialization BED').[78]

75. Competition Act, Art. 11 para. 2.
76. *Uredba o grupnom izuzeću vertikalnih sporazuma od zabrane, Službeni list Crne Gore* 13/14.
77. *Uredba o grupnom izuzeću od zabrane horizontalnih sporazuma o istraživanju i razvoju, Službeni list Crne Gore* 13/14.
78. *Uredba o grupnom izuzeću od zabrane horizontalnih sporazuma o specijalizaciji, Službeni list Crne Gore* 13/14.

- Decree on group exemption of the agreement on the distribution of spare parts and the servicing of motor vehicles.[79]
- Decree on group exemption of agreement in the insurance sector.[80]
- Decree on group exemption of the transfer of technology agreements (hereinafter 'Transfer technology BED').[81]
- Decree on the group exemption from the prohibition of agreements in road transport, rail and inland water transport and the consortium agreement on liner maritime transport.[82]

152. Apart from block exemption decrees, Ministry in charge of the competition is authorized to prescribe the content and the manner of submitting the request for an individual exemption. The Ministry has adopted the following rulebooks:

- Rulebook on criteria for determining the relevant market.[83]
- Rulebook on the content of the request for individual exemptions.[84]
- Rulebook on the form and content of the official identification of authorized persons and special authorization for inspection.[85]

153. The content of the legal acts mentioned above is described in more detail in the relevant sections of this monograph.

II. Guidelines

154. The Agency has not so far developed the practice to issue formal guidelines (in Montenegrin: *Smjernice*) which would regulate competition law issues. The aforementioned practice could be effective in advancing the protection of competition law. In any case, it would undoubtedly contribute to a better understanding of individual antitrust principles.

155. So far, the Agency has issued one formal guidance (in Montenegrin: *Uputstvo*). It is guidance on the content and method for merger notification procedures.[86]

---

79. *Uredba o grupnom izuzeću od zabrane sporazuma o distribuciji rezervnih dijelova i servisiranju motornih vozila, Službeni list Crne Gore* 13/14.
80. *Uredba o grupnom izuzeću od zabrane sporazuma u sektoru osiguranja, Službeni list Crne Gore* 52/14.
81. *Uredba o grupnom izuzeću od zabrane sporazuma o prenosu tehnologije, Službeni list Crne Gore* 59/14.
82. *Uredba o grupnom izuzeću od zabrane sporazuma u drumskom, željezničkom i saobraćaju u unutrašnjim vodama i sporazuma o konzorcijumu u linijskom pomorskom saobraćaju, Službeni list Crne Gore* 59/14.
83. *Pravilnik o načinu i kriterijumima utvrđivanja relevantnog tržišta Službeni list Crne Gore* 18/13.
84. *Pravilnik o sadržaju i načinu podnošenja zahtjeva za pojedinačno izuzeće sporazuma od zabrane, Službeni list Crne Gore* 18/13.
85. *Pravilnik o obliku i sadržaju službene identifikacije ovlašc´enih lica i posebnom ovlašc´enju za inspekciju, Službeni list Crne Gore 18/13.*
86. *Uputstvo o sadržaju i načinu podnošenja zahtjeva za izdavanje odobrenja za sprovođenje koncentracije, Službeni list Crne Gore* 44/12.

§4. Sources' Relation and Hierarchy

156. The relation between various sources of law and their hierarchy in Montenegro is precisely defined by the Constitution.

157. The highest source of law is the constitution, followed by confirmed international agreements. In the area of competition, the most important agreement is the SAA between Montenegro and the EU. After these acts, next in the hierarchy of the legal act are laws, followed by other regulations (decrees, rulebooks, guidelines).

158. Article 145 of the Constitution (Chapter VII on Constitutionality and Legality) sets out the general principle of hierarchy and conformity of legal acts in Montenegro. It provides a general principle that the law shall be in conformity with the Constitution and confirmed international agreements, and other regulations shall be in conformity with the Constitution and the law. Individual legal act shall be in conformity with the law.[87]

159. The Constitutional Court has jurisdiction to decide on the conformity of laws with the Constitution and confirmed and published international agreements as well as the conformity of other regulations and general acts with the Constitution and the law. Constitution has a provision that the Constitutional Court shall monitor the enforcement of constitutionality and legality and shall inform the Parliament about the noted cases of unconstitutionality and illegality.[88]

§5. Role and Authority of Precedents

160. As explained in an earlier chapter, legal order in Montenegro is based on continental legal tradition. Formally, court decisions do not represent the official source of law. In accordance with the Constitution, the court is autonomous and independent. The court shall rule on the basis of the Constitution, laws, and confirmed and published international agreements.[89]

161. In the part which regulates the Supreme Court, Constitutions set out the principle that the Supreme Court shall secure unified enforcement of laws by the courts.[90] Also, Law on Courts in detail regulates this issue by providing that the Supreme Court bench (in Montenegrin: *Opšta sjednica Vrhovnog suda*) shall adopt a principal legal position (in Montenegrin: *načelni pravni stav*) with a view to ensuring uniform application of the Constitution, laws and other regulations in the territory of Montenegro. Every court may request the adoption of or amendment to a

---

87. Constitution, Art. 148 para. 1.
88. *Id.*, Art. 149 para. 3.
89. *Id.*, Art. 118.
90. *Id.*, Art. 124 para. 1.

principle legal position. Principal positions, by their importance and authority of the institution, objectively have binding legal force, although they are formally not the legal basis for decision-making.

162. In practice, the role of precedents is reviewed by the court division, which can be established in all courts depending on the number of judges, scope and type of cases. The court division shall consider legal issues falling within its scope of work, take legal positions concerning issues falling within its competence, etc.[91] For the precedents, it is also worth mentioning the role of the session of judges which has authority to take legal positions concerning the cases falling within the jurisdiction of that court and deliver legal opinions relevant to case law.[92]

163. Additionally, it can be noted from the developments in jurisprudence that the role of precedents is increasing in practice. In practice, lower courts follow the views of a higher court and previous jurisprudence is being often quoted in submissions of the parties. This is a welcome change due to the fact that once when Montenegro enters the EU, Montenegrin courts will be required to follow the jurisprudence of the CJEU in competition law issues.

164. In relation to this issue, it is important to point out that the Agency provides interpretations of certain provisions of the law or ambiguities in its application, most often on the request of an interested party. It is clear from the Agency's annual reports that it is increasingly common for interested parties to contact the Agency regarding their situations, cases or actions, with the aim of using an official interpretation of the Agency to prevent the potential for distortion of competition in their individual. Although not formally a source of law, they represent the Agency's official position on specific issues and have value. It is especially affirmative that the excerpts from the opinions of the Agency are published in its annual reports. This creates a practice in the work of the Agency.

165. Finally, the Agency issues its decisions in the first instance in administrative proceedings. There is no imperative norm in legislation that obliges the Agency to follow its previous case law. However, so far based on analyses of the publicly available decisions, the Agency did not change its positions adopted in earlier cases.

91. Law on Courts, Arts 41 and 42.
92. *Id.*, Art. 40.

Chapter 2. Scope of Application

§1. Territorial Reach

166. Territorial scope is one of the basic provisions in the Competition Act, and one of the key principles of the EU competition law.

167. Competition law in Article 2 states:

> This Law shall apply to acts and practices done in the territory of Montenegro and/or to acts and practices occurring as a consequence of acts or practices done outside its territory which have as their object or effect the distortion of competition in the territory of Montenegro.

168. The first part of this article is, in practice, very clear; it limits the application of the law to acts and practices undertaken within the territory of Montenegro. The second part of the article can cause problems in the process of factual determination, whether acts undertaken outside of Montenegro have as their object or effect the distortion of competition in the territory of Montenegro.[93] For example, in some cases, in merger control regime, in practice, it is not clear enough on which base has the jurisdiction of Agency been determined. In some cases, foreign-to-foreign transactions are cleared by the Agency despite the fact that the subject transaction would not have any effect in Montenegro.

169. Agency has established practice that a merger requires its clearance whenever the relevant turnover thresholds prescribed in the Competition Act are exceeded, regardless of the merger's effects on the Montenegrin market.[94]

170. This situation requires careful examination, especially taking into account the number of these situations in practice. For example, according to the Agency's annual report for 2017, thirty-five requests for approval of concentrations have been submitted to the Agency in 2017. Out of this number, nine concentrations have been conducted within the territory of Montenegro, and other twenty-eight have been conducted outside of Montenegro.[95]

171. In the previous practice of the Agency based on the publicly available information, all infringement cases in areas of restrictive agreements and abuse of dominance have a connection to entities registered in Montenegro and to acts and practices done within the territory of Montenegro.

172. Also, it is not currently possible to verify information on whether the Agency has so far taken any initiative to initiate the procedure in such situations.

93. RaškoRadovanović, *Territorial Scope of Montenegrin Competition Law*, CEE Legal Matters, 63 (2017).
94. *See* Part III, Ch. 3, §1, I below.
95. Agency's Annual Report for 2017, p. 50.

As will be explained below, in Montenegrin law, the Agency formally issues a decision to initiate the procedure ex officio, when it assumes that there is an impairment of competition. Therefore, the initiative itself by the stakeholder does not imply an obligation on the Agency to formally and automatically initiate a procedure for an investigation into impairment of competition. From this point, it is difficult to explain how the Agency would evaluate the effect on the Montenegrin market for acts or practices done outside the territory of Montenegro.

§2. Special Sectors

173. The Competition Act regulates the protection of competition in the overall market of Montenegro, regardless of the economic sector. However, by sectorial pieces of legislation, some competencies of sectoral regulators concerning the protection of competition have been established. The most important is in the areas of banking, insurance, telecommunication, media and energy sector.

174. Technical regulation of the market is exclusively within the competence of the sector regulator. Sectoral regulators are the bearers of technical and other technological know-how, which the employed experts in the Agency usually do not possess, and in this sense, cooperation is in the best public interest. In the previous period, cooperation with regulators was reflected in the mutual flow of data and information for the needs of concentrations, sectoral analyses and determination of the abuse of the dominant position of market participants whose activity is under the competence of the regulators. In some cases which will be elaborated, there is close cooperation established by the sectoral legislation (e.g., in the sector of electronic communications). However, in other cases, there is no strict obligation for cooperation established by the sectoral laws. For example, regulation in the financial market sector does not contain the precisely defined obligation of cooperation between regulators and the Agency (but it exists in practice). Finally, in some cases is evident the lack of will for the establishment of closer cooperation, due to the various factors.

I. Electronic Communications

175. Law on Electronic Communication (hereinafter 'LEC') regulates the manner of management and use of electronic communications networks, terms and manner of conducting the activities in the area of electronic communications and other matters pertaining to electronic communications.[96] By the LEC, an independent regulatory body Agency for Electronic Communications and Postal Services is established (in Montenegrin: *Agencija za elektronske komunikacije i poštansku djelatnost*, hereinafter 'AECPS'),[97] with jurisdiction *inter alia* to analyse relevant

96. LEC (*Zakon o elektronskim komunikacijama, Službeni list Crne Gore* 040/13, 056/13, 002/17).
97. Website available at (in English): http://www.ekip.me/eng/ (last accessed 11 Oct. 2019).

markets, determine operators with significant market power and take regulatory measures to prevent the negative effects of significant market power of operators.[98]

176. AECPS identifies relevant markets susceptible to *ex ante* regulation. LEC prescribes that in the procedure for identification, monitoring and analyses of relevant markets on the electronic communications market in Montenegro, the AECPS shall cooperate with the body competent for protection of competition.[99] The Agency has concluded the Protocol on cooperation with the AECPS.

177. In accordance with LEC, a market susceptible to *ex ante* regulation shall be the market having structural, regulatory and other lasting barriers which prevent the market entry of new competitors and where it is impossible to develop competition without *ex ante* regulation. *Ex ante* regulation includes defining special conditions under which the operators with significant market power carry on the activity of electronic communications for the purpose of ensuring market competition development.[100]

178. Operators with significant market power fall under special regulation. For the purpose of LEC, an operator shall be deemed to have significant market power if, *either individually or jointly with other operators, it enjoys a position of economic strength affording it the power to behave to an appreciable extent independently of its competitors and users.*[101] In the market analysis procedure, the AECPS have right to: (1) identify relevant markets susceptible to *ex ante* regulation; (2) define relevant markets and assess the existence of one or more operators with significant market power in order to assess whether the relevant market is effectively competitive; (3) impose regulatory obligations on the operators with significant market power if the analysed relevant market is not effectively competitive; (4) withdraw all regulatory obligations from the operators with significant market power if the analysed relevant market is effectively competitive.[102] For example, according to available data, in 2017, the AECPS conducted a process of analysis of five relevant markets in line with the European Commission Recommendation on relevant markets subject to prior regulation (2014/10/EU).

179. If on the basis of market analysis, the AECPS finds that the market lacks sufficient competition, it shall identify an operator and/or operators with significant market power in that market.[103] The AECPS is obliged to request an opinion from the Agency before identification of an operator and/or operators with significant market power.

98. LEC, Art. 11.
99. *Id.*, Art. 65 para. 1.
100. *Id.*, Art. 63.
101. *Id.*, Art. 67 para. 1.
102. *Id.*, Art. 64.
103. *Id.*, Art. 69 para. 1.

180. AECPS can impose on the operator with significant market power, one or more measures prescribed by the LEC. It could be the following measures: (1) obligation to disclose information;[104] (2) change in reference offer;[105] (3) obligation of non-discrimination;[106] (4) accounting separation;[107] (5) enabling access to, and use of, network elements and associated facilities;[108] (6) price control and cost accounting;[109] (7) regulation of retail service prices.[110] For example, according to available data from 2018, based on the AECPS decision on lowering the prices of voice telephony and broadband Internet access, Crnogorski Telekom, the largest telecommunication provider, lowered the prices of telephone calls and monthly subscription fees for the telephone and the Internet for the fourth time in five years.[111]

II. Energy Sector

181. The energy sector of Montenegro is one of the main pillars of the national economy. The development of the energy sector is defined by Energy development strategy of Montenegro by 2030. The main objective set by the Strategy is to ensure sustainable, safe and competitive supply of all energy sources together with energy efficiency measures and increased utilization of renewable energy sources.

182. Law on Energy regulates terms and conditions for carrying out energy activities, the procedure for organization and management of the electricity and gas market as well as other matters of relevance for the energy sector.[112] This Law established the Energy Regulatory Agency (in Montenegrin: *Regulatorna agencija za energetiku*, hereinafter 'REA') as an independent regulator of the energy sector.[113]

183. REA has jurisdiction to perform direct monitoring over the functioning of electricity and gas market and impose measures for elimination of identified deficiencies in market functioning. REA is obliged by the Law on Energy to cooperate with the body competent for competition, financial market regulators and the competent Community's body during research related to competition issues.

104. *Id.*, Art. 71.
105. *Id.*, Art. 72.
106. *Id.*, Art. 73.
107. *Id.*, Art. 74.
108. *Id.*, Art. 75.
109. *Id.*, Art. 76.
110. *Id.*, Art. 78.
111. AECPS Annual Report for 2017, available at: http://www.ekip.me/izvjestaji/oradu.php (last accessed 11 Oct. 2019).
112. Law on Energy (*Zakon o energetici, Službeni list Crne Gore* 5/2016, 51/2017).
113. Website available at (in English): http://regagen.co.me/site_en/ (last accessed 11 Oct. 2019).

184. The basic principle of the Law is that prices of electricity and gas shall be freely established on the organized market or bilaterally in a contract between sellers and buyers.[114] However, the Law requires for regulation the following prices in energy sector: (1) use of electricity and gas transmission and distribution systems; (2) use of gas storage systems and transport and storage of liquefied natural gas facilities; (3) provision of ancillary services and services for balancing of transmission electricity or gas system; (4) a charge for operation of Market Operator.

III. Financial Market Sector

185. In the financial sector, several regulators, directly or indirectly, deal with competition law issues.

186. The CBM is the regulatory body in the banking sector,[115] which is established and regulated by the Law on Central bank of Montenegro (hereinafter 'LCBM').[116] In accordance with LCBM, the main objective of the CBM shall be to foster and maintain the financial system stability, including fostering and maintaining a sound banking system and safe and efficient payment systems. CBM should contribute to achieving and maintaining price stability.[117]

187. Law on Banks has a general norm, which contains restriction of impairment of competition.[118] Law on Banks deals with competition law issues in the determination of qualified participation in a bank, restrictions of mutual investments, deciding on granting the approval for acquiring qualified participation, the concentration at the banking market, etc.

188. The role of the CBM in the scope of competition law is also connected mainly on giving consent to a merger of two or more banks or to the division of a bank.

189. In accordance with Law on Banks, CBM shall deny the granting of approval for the acquisition of qualified participation in a bank if the granting of approval would lead to the concentration of the participants at the financial market which significantly prevents, restricts or violates the competition, primarily through the creation or strengthening of dominant position at the financial market.[119]

190. In the previous year, the subject of attention regarding competition law was that CBM granted approval for qualifying holding-in share capital in the merger of the two largest banks in Montenegro – Crnogorska komercijalna banka AD Podgorica and Societe Generale Bank Montenegro. Crnogorska komercijalna banka

114. Law on Energy, Art. 58.
115. Website available at (in English): https://www.cbcg.me/en. (last accessed 11 Oct. 2019).
116. LCBM (*Zakon o Centralnoj banci Crne Gore*, *Službeni list Crne Gore* 40/10, 46/10, 6/13, 70/17).
117. *Id.*, Art. 4.
118. Law on Banks (*Zakon o bankama, Službeni list Crne Gore* 17/08, 44/10, 40/11, 73/17).
119. *Id.*, Art. 12.

AD Podgorica, operating within the Hungarian OTP Group, submitted to the CBM on 27 March 2019, a request for authorization to acquire qualifying holding of 90.5% in the share capital of Societe Generale Bank Montenegro AD. This procedure was carried out in cooperation with the Agency since the approval for the acquisition of qualifying holding provided by the CBM under the Law on Banks was preceded by the procedure for approval of concentration in accordance with the Competition Act. Also, in the procedure for approval of the concentration before the Agency, the Agency cooperates with the CBM, as a regulator in the banking market. In this procedure, based on the analysis of data obtained from CBM, as a regulator in the relevant market of the parties to the concentration, the Agency determined that the concentration in question will not prevent, restrict or distort effective competition, that is, create or strengthen a dominant position within the established relevant market.[120]

191. Law on Banks has instituted *undesirable concentration in the banking market.* In the context of the Law on Banks, the undesirable concentration in banking market shall be bank restructuring through amalgamation or other actions if such restructuring or actions materially prevent, limit or violate competition in the banking market. Law set up the main criteria for determining undesirable concentration. They are as follows: (1) share of total balance sheet assets of the individual bank in total balance sheet assets of all banks in Montenegro, (2) share of bank assets in total assets of banks in Montenegro, (3) share of a bank in market coverage with individual products and services, (4) the concentration of bank's credit activities to certain target groups, (5) other criteria important for determining undesirable concentration at the financial market.[121] The CBM has not had the opportunity so far to determine the undesirable concentration in the banking sector.

192. For the insurance market, the competent regulatory body is the Insurance Supervision Agency (in Montenegrin: *Agencija za nadzor osiguranja*, hereinafter 'ISA'). ISA is established by the Insurance Law.[122] ISA gives prior consent for the acquisition of shares to a person who intends to acquire, directly or indirectly, a qualifying holding in an insurance company (10% of shares or voting rights).[123] The Agency has concluded the Protocol in cooperation with the ISA.

193. In practice so far, with regards to the dispute conducted by the Agency in the case of Sava Osiguranje, there has been a contrary interpretation of ISA in relation to the position of the Agency. More information on this dispute in a separate section of the monograph.

---

120. *See* Agency Decision No. 04-UPI-23/14-19 of 23 Apr. 2019, available at: http://www.azzk.me/1/doc/koncentracije/2019/2019-04-23_CKB-SG%20Bank%20MNE.pdf (last accessed 11 Oct. 2019).
121. Law on Banks, Art. 77.
122. Insurance Law (*Zakon o osiguranju, Službeni list Republike Crne Gore* 078/06, 053/09, 073/10, 040/11, 055/16).
123. *Id.*, Art. 23.

194. Commission for the capital market (in Montenegrin: *Komisija za tržište kapitala*) is the regulatory body for the capital market in Montenegro. Commission for the capital market is established by the Law on Capital Market.[124] This Law has a general norm, which prevents the market operator from unfair competition or the introduction of unjustified restrictions on market entry.[125] So far, no cooperation has been established between this regulator and the Agency.

IV. Media

195. For a market of 660,000 inhabitants (comprising about 220,000 households), the concentration of media in Montenegro is relatively high: four daily newspapers, a national public media service with two television stations and two radio channels, fourteen local public-service radio stations, thirty-six private radio stations, three local public-service television stations, fourteen private television stations. What is striking is the economic weakness of most of these media outlets, which would not survive without receiving various types of assistance from the state.[126]

196. One of the first cases of establishing a cartel agreement on the Montenegrin market was the agreement on the price-fixing in the daily newspapers market.[127] Competition law issues are present in the media sector, mostly through control of concentration in the media sector. Development of competition is one of the main principles established by the Electronic media law (hereinafter 'EML'). EML prohibits the broadcasting of programmes which violate provisions on media concentration or the antimonopoly provisions.[128] The Agency for Electronic Media (in Montenegrin: *Agencija za elektronske medije* (hereinafter 'AEM') is the regulatory body in the sector of performing the activity of production and provision of audiovisual media services.[129]

197. One of the most problematic issues to deal in practice in the media sector in Montenegro is the existence of the unlawful media concentration. In accordance with Article 131 of the EML, unlawful media concentration exists in situations when a broadcaster:

(1) holding a licence for national coverage broadcasting: (i) holds a stake in the founding capital of another broadcaster with such licence with more than 25% share of capital or voting rights, (ii) holds more than a 10% stake in the founding capital of a legal entity publishing daily print media with the circulation exceeding 3,000 copies, or vice versa, (iii) holds more than a 10% stake in the

124. Law on Capital Market (*Zakon o tržištu kapitala, Službeni list Crne Gore* 001/18).
125. *Id.*, Art. 150.
126. Željko Rutović, *Media Regulation in Montenegro*, Media dialogues, 7, 13 (2010).
127. *See* Part II, Ch. 1, §1, I, A below.
128. EML (*Zakon o elektronskim medijima, Službeni list Crne Gore* 046/10, 040/11, 053/11, 006/13, 055/16, 092/17).
129. Website available at (in English): http://aemcg.org/en/ (last accessed 11 Oct. 2019).

founding capital of a legal entity performing the activity of a news agency and vice versa, (iv) concurrently publishes the daily print media with the circulation exceeding 3,000 copies;

(2) except the national public broadcaster, broadcasts more than one television and one radio programme with the same or similar programme base over the same area;

(3) radio or television programme licensed for broadcasting with local or regional coverage: (i) holds more than 30% stake in the founding capital of another broadcaster with regional or local coverage over the same area; (ii) concurrently, over the same or in neighbouring areas, publishes local daily print media.

198. The AEM will not grant a broadcasting licence if it is established that its granting would lead to unlawful media concentration.[130] Several times, AEM has had successful interventions in preventing unlawful media concentration.

199. AEM is obliged by the EML to cooperate with the administrative body responsible for competition as regards electronic communications market analysis which constitutes a requirement for the provision of and/or access to audiovisual media services.[131] At the end of 2017, AEM signed a Memorandum of Cooperation with the Agency, based on Article 11 of the Law on Electronic Media and Article 37 of the Competition Act. The Memorandum regulates the cooperation of the two agencies in reviewing the situation and conducting analysis and market research of audiovisual media services and electronic communications services. The Agency, in 2017, twice contacted the AEM with the request for the submission of data and opinions necessary for the implementation of the procedure for analysing the conditions of competition in the market of production, sale and distribution of media content in the territory of Montenegro through various technologies. The proceedings were conducted on the initiative of the company Radio Difuzni Centar for the examination of the violation of competition by Telemach and M-tel due to potential violations of competition by the company, Total TV Montenegro. The AEM has provided all relevant information at its disposal.[132]

V. Other Legislation

200. In addition to the aforementioned laws, in the legal system of Montenegro other individual laws also regulate, directly or indirectly, issues in the area of competition law. For example, the Law on Internal Trade regulates the issue of unfair competition.[133] Unfair competition, for the purposes of this Law, shall be contrary

130. EML, Art. 134 para. 1.
131. *Id.*, Art. 11.
132. AEM Annual Report for 2017, available at: http://aemcg.org/wp-content/uploads/2018/05/Izvje%C5%A1taj-o-radu-AEM-za-2017.-godinu.pdf. (last accessed 11 Oct. 2019).
133. Law on Internal Trade (*Zakon o unutrašnjoj trgovini, Službeni list Crne Gore* 049/08, 040/11, 038/19).

to such trader's activities which, contrary to the good business practice, are or may be detrimental to other traders or the buyer. Examples of unfair competition set in this Law include, *inter alia*, the following activities: (1) advertising, announcement, or offering of goods by indicating the data or using the expressions which create or may create misconceptions on the market about such goods; (2) telling untruths about other traders that are detrimental to his reputation and business; (3) the sale of goods with marks or data which are or may be thinking of the trader in respect of the origin, method of production, quantity, quality, or other properties of the goods; (4) concealing the flaws of goods or otherwise misleading the buyer; (5) taking actions focused on the termination of business relationships between other traders or aimed at preventing or impeding such relationships etc.[134] According to publicly available information, often due to issues in the area of internal trade, which are the responsibility of inspections, parties turn to the Agency to initiate proceedings for establishing impairment of competition.

201. Certain behaviours that constitute unfair competition in Montenegrin law are subject to the attention of competent inspections and do not fall within the competence of the Agency. More specifically, when certain actions which, under sectoral laws constitute unfair competition, abuse a dominant position on the market or create a restrictive agreement, there is an obligation on the Agency to initiate a procedure for determining the abuse of competition. The best example of this is the practice of dumping. In accordance with the Foreign Trade Law,[135] dumping is the importation of goods into the Republic at less than their normal value, under conditions that cause or threaten to cause material injury to an industry established in the Republic or materially retards the establishment of an industry in Montenegro.[136] In such cases, the competent authority shall conduct an investigation on the basis of a written application made by, or on behalf of, the domestic industry. Also, in this situation, the Government may levy an anti-dumping duty provided that it has been established on the basis of investigations that: (1) there has been a significant increase in dumped or subsidized imports compared to the level of domestic production or consumption; and (2) there has been significant price undercutting by the dumped or subsidized imports compared to the price of the like domestic products, or the prices of such imported products have depressed to a significant degree the price of the like product, or have prevented that price from increasing as it would otherwise have done; and (3) as a result, material injury is caused to the domestic industry, or there is a threat of such injury to the domestic industry.[137]

202. The Agency has no authority to enforce the procedure and/or to initiate a penalty procedure in the event of price dumping by any market participant. However, the Agency has the authority to conduct proceedings against those market participants who would determine the extremely low price for a certain product with

134. *Id.*, Art. 40.
135. Foreign Trade Law (*Zakon o spoljnoj trgovini, Službeni list Crne Gore* 028/04, 037/07, 073/10, 057/14).
136. *Id.*, Art. 35 para. 1 item 1.
137. *Id.*, Art. 36 para. 1 items 1–3.

the aim of expelling existing competitors from the market or discouraging potential competitors from entering the Montenegrin market. Such a predatory act is punishable.

203. Also, in certain sectors of the industry, Montenegro regulates prices through laws and/or by-laws.

204. For example, the Law on Medicines stipulates that the Government of Montenegro shall establish criteria for determining maximum prices of medicines used in human medicine and are prescribed and issued as a burden of compulsory health insurance.[138] This issue is regulated in detail by a separate Regulation – the Regulation on Criteria for the Formation of Maximum Drug Prices.[139]

205. The Postal Services Act provides that postal services shall not contain additional amounts due to considerable market power of a postal operator in the postal services market.[140] Also, postal services prices shall not be set below cost in order to retrieve or retain significant market power in the postal services market. Universal postal service prices are determined by the postal operator according to the criteria established by the AECPS. The prices of the universal postal service are approved by the AECPS, not later than thirty days after the delivery of the price list.

206. The maximum prices of oil and petroleum products are regulated by the decree on the methods for the formation of maximum retail prices for petroleum products.[141] Law on Road Transport Safety stipulates that the amount of the cost of taking the driving test shall be determined by the Government at the proposal of the state administration authority in charge of education.[142] Driving schools have been the subject of the Agency's attention in the case of inspecting impairment of competition.[143]

207. The Law on Utility Services provides that the municipality, i.e., the Government, shall regulate the manner and conditions for organizing and conducting utilities.[144] The law stipulates that the municipality or the Government of Montenegro shall approve the price list for the provision of utility services, that is, for the delivery of a utility product.[145]

---

138. Law on Medicines (*Zakon o ljekovima, Službeni list Crne Gore* 056/11, 006/13).
139. *Uredba o kriterijumima za formiranje maksimalnih cijena ljekova, Službeni list Crne Gore* 44/2015 and 65/2015.
140. Postal Services Act (*Zakon o poštanskim uslugama, Službeni list Crne Gore* 057/11, 055/16, 055/18).
141. *Uredba o načinu obrazovanja maksimalnih maloprodajnih cijena naftnih derivata, Službeni list Republike Crne Gore* 52/02, 23/03, 35/05, 73/08, 73/10.
142. Law on Road Transport Safety (*Zakon o bezbjednosti saobraćaja na putevima, Službeni list Crne Gore* 033/12, 058/14, 014/17).
143. *See* Part II, Ch. 1, §1, I, A below.
144. Law on Utility Services (*Zakon o komunalnim djelatnostima, Službeni list Crne Gore* 055/16, 074/16 and 002/18).
145. *Id.*, Art. 29 para. 2.

§3. State-Owned Enterprises and Public Utilities

208. The Competition Act applies to all legal subjects (legal and natural persons) engaged in economic activity, regardless of the person's legal status, form of ownership, registered address, nationality or residence.[146]

209. In the practice of applying the 2006 Competition Act, the application of the law to companies which perform the business activity of public interest was controversial. Administration for Protection of Competition has investigated the impairment of competition in several cases, but the Administrative Court annulled the decisions finding the impairment of competition on the grounds that the 2006 Competition Act did not apply to them.

210. This was one of the arguments because of which the Competition Act now has an explicit norm which determines its application to undertakings performing activities of public interest.

211. It is clearly based on the provision that this Act applies to state-owned enterprises and public utilities. However, due to the fact that the Montenegrin legal system does not contain clear provisions regarding state-owned enterprises, several important facts need to be highlighted.

212. Public company as separate legal person with defined legal status, structure and purpose does not exist in Montenegro. After the adoption of the Company Act in 2002, so-called *public companies* were not a part of the Montenegrin legal system.[147] Companies established by the government or municipalities have a specific legal regime. However, these companies are established in the legal forms set out by the Company Act. In a formally legal manner and substantially, these companies have the same rights, obligations and organization as other business organizations.

213. Hence, some companies still keep in their name *public company* (in Montenegrin: *javno preduzeće*).

214. During the 1990s and beginning 2000s, this type of company was common in the Montenegrin legal system and was regulated by the Federal Law on Public Enterprises.[148] This Law defined public enterprises as the *enterprise conducting economic activity which is an indispensable precondition for normal living and working conditions of Montenegrin citizens or for the work of other enterprises or administrative bodies*. The definition itself shows that apart from being oriented

146. *This Law shall apply to legal and natural persons engaged in an economic activity and participating in the production of and trade in goods and/or services in the territory of Montenegro.* Article 3 para. 1 Competition Act.

147. Company Act (*Zakon o privrednim društvima, Službeni list Crne Gore* 006/02, 017/07, 080/08, 040/10, 036/11 and 040/11).

148. Law on Public Enterprises (*Zakon o javnim preduzećima, Official Gazette of the Socialist Republic of Montenegro* 6/91).

towards accruing profit, public enterprises have the prevailing purpose of performing publicly important service, such as providing electricity, water supply, organizing parking service, etc. This obviously adds the term *non-commercial* as an adjective to these entities.

215. The Law on Utility Services provides, *inter alia*, for the following utilities: (1) public water supply; (2) municipal wastewater management; (3) atmospheric water management; (4) municipal waste management; (5) landscaping and maintenance of public areas; (6) managing public lighting; (7) public transportation of passengers in urban and suburban areas; (8) maintenance of municipal roads (local roads, city streets and streets in settlements) and bicycle lanes; (9) maintenance of the riverbed of local importance; (10) maintenance of public cemeteries, chapels and crematoriums and burial; (11) market maintenance; (12) maintenance of public parking spaces, etc.[149] The subject of investigation of the competition authorities were utility services in the areas of public transport of passengers in urban and suburban settlements and the maintenance of public cemeteries, chapels, crematoriums and burial.[150]

216. Utility services may be performed by the following legal entities: (1) a company established by a local government unit; (2) a privately owned company or entrepreneur; (3) a company majority-owned by the Government and established by the Government; (4) a company with the capacity of a legal entity jointly founded by the Government and local self-government unit/s.[151] Utilities have been the subject of attention in several cases of abuse of a dominant position. One of the most significant cases of abuse of a dominant position in the Agency's practices to date has been that of a utility company. This is the case of Budva Vodovod, which will be further described in a separate section of the monograph.[152]

217. The Competition Act also applies to undertakings to whom the right to perform a particular activity was conferred by an act of a competent public body. This can be avoided if the application of Competition Act would considerably obstruct the performance of such activities. The burden of proof lies with the undertaking performing such activity.[153] Also, in Montenegro, there is no single legislative act regulating public institutions as the specific type of entities providing public service. Hence, different types of institutions – sometimes even a single institution – are regulated by specific laws. Such legislation which also applies to public institutions exists in the fields of education, health, social care, culture, sport, etc. These

149. Law on Utility Services, Art. 2 para. 1.
150. *See* Part II, Ch. 2, §1, I below.
151. Law on Utility Services, Art. 20 para. 1.
152. *See* Part II, Ch. 2, §1, I, C below.
153. Competition Act, Art. 5 para. 2.

institutions can also be directly or indirectly involved in performing some kind of economic activities and fall under the application of the Competition Act.[154]

§4. Sensible Effect and *De Minimis*

218. Impairment of competition may occur when an undertaking performs an act (in Montenegrin: *akt*) or an action (in Montenegrin: *radnja*) which has or may have as its object or effect significant restriction, distortion or prevention of competition.

219. According to Article 8 of the Competition Act which covers the general prohibition of restrictive agreements in Montenegrin competition law, agreements which have as their *object or effect* the prevention, restriction or distortion of competition on the territory of Montenegro are prohibited. Concentrations between undertakings are generally permitted unless *they are creating a new dominant position or strengthening a dominant position of one or more undertakings, either separately or in combination, which may significantly affect prevention, restriction or distortion of effective competition in the relevant market.*[155]

220. Article 101 of the TFEU prohibits agreements between companies which have as their object or effect of restricting competition within the Single Market. The CJEU has consistently held that Article 101 TFEU is not applicable where the impact of an agreement on competition is not appreciable. Montenegrin competition law has introduced the institute of agreements of minor significance (*de minimis* agreements).

221. The Competition Act defines agreements of minor significance as agreements between undertakings whose aggregate market share in the relevant market of products and services does not exceed:

(1) 10% market share, where the agreement is concluded between undertakings operating at the same level of production or trade (horizontal agreements);
(2) 15% market share, where the agreement is concluded between undertakings operating at different levels of production or trade (vertical agreements);
(3) 10% share on a relevant market for the agreements where it is not clearly defined whether those are horizontal or vertical agreements.

222. The general rule is that *de minimis* agreements are not prohibited. However, the Competition Act sets three exceptions. The *de minimis* rule does not apply to agreements which: (1) directly or indirectly fix purchase or selling prices or any

154. *This Law shall also apply to undertakings performing activities of public interest and to those to whom the right to perform a particular activity was conferred by an act of a competent public body insofar as the application of this Law would not considerably obstruct the performance of such activities.* Competition Act, Art. 5.
155. Competition Act, Art. 18 para. 1.

other trading conditions, (2) limit or control production, market, technical development or investment; (3) share markets or sources of supply.

223. In the practice of the Agency's work, for now, this legal institute has not been used. Also, the Agency has not adopted any guidelines on the application of these exceptions to the *de minimis* rule.

Chapter 3. Overview of Substantive Provisions

§1. Restrictive Agreements

224. Restrictive agreements are regulated in Article 8 of the Competition Act. This article is harmonized with Article 101(1) TFEU and has for the first time introduced in the Montenegrin legal system new broader definition of the restrictive agreements. Montenegrin competition law prohibits all acts which have as their *object or effect* the prevention, restriction or distortion of competition in the relevant market.

225. The definition of restrictive agreement in Article 8 of the Competition Act has three elements. First, it introduced the general principle that restrictive agreements are prohibited and shall be null and void. Second, this article specified forms of restrictive agreements as *written or verbal arrangements, agreements, contracts, single provisions of agreements, explicit or tacit agreements, concerted practice, as well as decisions by associations of undertakings*. Third, it defines concrete actions in restrictive agreements. These are agreements which:

(1) directly or indirectly fix purchase or selling prices or any other trading conditions;
(2) limit or control production, market, technical development or investment;
(3) share markets or sources of supply;
(4) apply dissimilar conditions to equivalent transactions with different undertakings, thereby placing them at a competitive disadvantage;
(5) make the conclusion of agreements subject to acceptance by the other parties of supplementary obligations which, by their nature or according to commercial usage, have no connection with the subject of such agreements;
(6) impose the obligation to apply particular resale price or otherwise ensure the application of recommended resale price.[156]

226. Furthermore, Article 8 contains an explanation of the meaning of concerted practice which means cooperation between undertakings which, without having concluded a formal or informal agreement, is aimed at coordination of business activities of competitors in the relevant market, which can be achieved by direct or indirect contact between undertakings and which is not a consequence of regular economic activity and independent operation of undertakings.

227. Restrictive agreement can be horizontal and vertical. Horizontal restrictive agreements cover agreements between existing and/or potential undertakings operating at the same level of the production or distribution chain. Vertical restrictive agreements cover agreements on conditions of supply, purchase, sale or resale,

156. *Id.*, Art. 8.

between existing and/or potential undertakings operating at a different level of the production or distribution chain.[157] In all cases so far, the Agency investigated horizontal agreements.

§2. Dominant Undertakings

228. The Montenegrin Competition Act defines dominant undertakings based on several elements which cover dominant undertakings. First, it set as a principle that an undertaking has a dominant position in a relevant market if it has no competitors. Second, when the undertaking has significant market power enabling it to restrict or prevent the development of effective competition in the market of Montenegro or a part thereof. Third, if it has a significantly better position in relation to competitors enabling it to undertake business activities to a significant extent independently of its competitors, suppliers, buyers or end-users.[158]

229. In determining the dominant position, the Agency shall, in particular, take into account the following elements:

(1) market share and market power;
(2) level of concentration of the market, market shares and market power of competitors;
(3) market dynamics in the past period;
(4) financial power;
(5) buyers' power;
(6) access to sources of supply and demand;
(7) links with other undertakings in the relevant and connected markets;
(8) legal or other barriers to entry for other undertakings;
(9) the ability of the undertaking to dictate market conditions considering its supply and demand.

230. It remains to be seen how the Agency will evaluate the aforementioned factors when assessing dominance. Even though the market share thresholds create a legal presumption, such a presumption may be rebutted. In practice, market share is important, but not essentially the crucial indicator of dominance. Also, in the process of analysing market shares, attention must be paid to its absolute and relative rate as well as its changes in a certain period of time. Market share is primarily used at the beginning of proceedings for orientation purposes, and its relevance is established together with other factors.

231. The Competition Act has defined a market share threshold which determines whether an undertaking is dominant. It is presumed that an undertaking has a dominant position in the market of products (goods or services) if its market share

157. *Id.*, Art. 10.
158. *Id.*, Art. 14 para. 1.

in the relevant market exceeds 50%.[159] Dominance can be held collectively by two or more legally independent undertakings if there is no significant competition between them and if their aggregate share in the relevant market exceeds 60%.[160] The burden of proof that an undertaking whose share in the relevant market is lower than 50%, or lower than 60% in case of collective domination, can have a dominant position in the market with the Agency.[161] The Agency so far has not identified the practice of collective dominant position.

§3. CONCENTRATIONS

232. Montenegrin competition law in Article 16 regulates three situations which fall under the concentration of undertakings:

(1) the merger of two or more independent undertakings or parts thereof in the relevant market;[162]
(2) the acquisition, by one or more natural persons already controlling at least one undertaking, or by one or more undertakings, of indirect or direct control of the whole or a part of another undertaking;[163]
(3) a joint venture by two or more undertakings aimed at creating a new undertaking or acquiring joint control of the existing undertaking which operates independently on a lasting basis and performs all the functions of an autonomous undertaking.[164]

233. A detailed explanation of these three forms of concentration is provided in Part I, Chapter 4, §7 below.

234. However, the Competition Act regulates three situations where the acquisition of control shall not be considered to be the concentration of undertakings.

235. First, there is no concentration if a bank or other financial institution acquires shares or other securities in a certain undertaking on a temporary basis with a view to resell them, provided that it sells them no later than twelve months from the date of acquisition and that during the period in which it disposes of such securities, the ownership right is not used in order to influence the undertaking's business decisions that concern the competitive behaviour of that undertaking or provided that it uses such ownership right only with a view to preparing the sale of those securities or the assets of the undertaking.[165] Upon the acquirer's request that

159. *Id.*, Art. 14 para. 2.
160. *Id.*, Art. 14 para. 3.
161. *Id.*, Art. 14 para. 4.
162. *Id.*, Art. 16 para. 1 item 1.
163. *Id.*, Art. 16 para. 1 item 2.
164. *Id.*, Art. 16 para. 1 item 3.
165. *Id.*, Art. 17 para. 1 item 1.

demonstrates that the sale of securities was not reasonably possible within the period of twelve months, the Agency may extend the period for resale up to six months.[166]

236. Second, there is no concentration if the control of an undertaking is acquired by a person performing the duty of bankruptcy or liquidation trustee pursuant to the law regulating bankruptcy or liquidation.[167]

237. Third, there is no concentration if a joint venture has as its object the coordination of market activities between two or more undertakings that remain independent. However, such joint ventures are assessed under the provisions of the Competition Act on restrictive agreements.[168]

§4. Other Prohibitions

238. By signing SAA, Montenegro undertakes to establish an operationally independent authority entrusted with the powers necessary for the applicable provisions concerning full compliance of state aid with the EU regulations. For that purpose, Montenegro has established the State aid control commission (Montenegrin: *Komisija za kontrolu drzavne pomoći*) and the Division for preparation of state aid (Montenegrin: *Odjeljenje za pripremu državne pomoći*), an organizational unit of the Ministry of Finance which carries out professional, technical and administrative affairs for the Commission. The first law in Montenegro governing the state aid preparation, award and control was the Law on Control of State Support and Aid.[169] The Law on State Aid Control (in Montenegrin: *Zakon o kontroli državne pomoći,* hereinafter 'LSAC') is the second law adopted by Montenegro in this field.[170]

239. By adopting the LSAC, the state aid affairs were transferred to the competence of the Agency for the protection of competition, by amending the Competition Act in 2018.[171] In accordance with this Law, it was necessary to amend the Competition Act. Since 2018, the Agency is obliged to carry out the control of the compatibility of state aid with the law and of proper use of the allocated state aid. Also, the Agency has the power to order recovery of the unlawful and incompatible state aid.[172]

---

166. *Id.*, Art. 17 para. 2.
167. *Id.*, Art. 17 para. 1 item 2.
168. *Id.*, Art. 17 para. 1 item 3.
169. Law on Control of State Support and aid (*Zakon o kontroli državne podrške i pomoći, Službeni list Crne Gore* 26/07).
170. LSAC (*Zakon o kontroli državne pomoći, Službeni list Crne Gore* 74/09, 57/11).
171. Law on Amendments to the Law on Protection of Competition (*Zakon o izmjenama i dopunama Zakona o zaštiti konkurencije, Službeni list Crne Gore* 013/18).
172. LSAC, Art. 5 para. 1.

240. In accordance with the Competition Act, the Agency has the following jurisdiction in relation to state aid affairs:

- exercise the control of compliance of the State aid with the law regulating State aid (*ex ante* control);[173]
- exercise the control of compliance of the award and use of granted State aid with the law regulating State aid (*ex post* control);[174]
- monitor the implementation and the effects of the granted State aid;[175]
- order recovery of unlawful and non-compliant State aid;[176]
- collect and process data on planned State aid;[177]
- collect data on the use and effects of granted State aid;[178]
- submit an annual report to the Government and the Parliament of Montenegro (on granted state aid);[179]
- submit an annual report to the European Commission on granted State aid;
- give opinions at the request of a state administration body, competent local self-government body and a legal person managing and disposing of the funds from public revenues and state property in accordance with the law in the process of drafting of legislation and other acts regulating matters related to the award of state aid, as well as in the process of their adoption.[180]

241. Hence, from the above, it can be concluded that these are significant powers and obligations that require special expertise. The delegation of these obligations to the Agency makes room for the question of whether competition law issues will be neglected in the future in the work of the Agency. State aid in Montenegrin law has become an object of attention due to a number of cases that have been of interest to the general public. In addition, the Agency's capacities, especially in the area of expert staff, are limited. The time ahead will show whether this decision was right.

242. There are no other prohibitions in the Montenegrin competition law.

§5. Test of Illegality

I. Per Se Prohibition and Naked Restrictions

243. The Montenegrin law recognizes the object-effect dichotomy. This means that certain acts fall within Article 8 of the Competition Act per se. However, the Agency needs to establish an adverse effect on competition in order for the other

173. Competition Act, Art. 19 para. 1 item 5.
174. *Id.*, Art. 19 para. 1 item 6.
175. *Id.*, Art. 19 para. 1 item 7.
176. *Id.*, Art. 19 para. 1 item 8.
177. *Id.*, Art. 19 para. 1 item 9.
178. *Id.*, Art. 19 para. 1 item 10.
179. *Id.*, Art. 19 para. 1 item 12.
180. *Id.*, Art. 19 para. 1 item 14.

acts to fall within the application of Article 8. It is not always clear whether an agreement or practice will be treated by the Agency as being restrictive by its object or by its effect. Also, neither the Competition Act nor the Agency developed any criteria for the distinction between these two types of restrictions.

244. Based on publicly available information, the focus of the Agency so far has been on restriction by objects. In the practice of the Agency, which is confirmed by the court decisions, it is not needed to show effects in case of object type restrictions. For example, in the rationale of the judgment of the Administrative Court in *Sava Montenegro and Lovćen osiguranje*, it is stated that in the proceedings establishing the existence of cartel agreements within the meaning of Article 8 of the Competition Act, it is not necessary to prove the existence of the effects or adverse consequences of the agreements in question in each case, but the harmfulness of such acts is presumed by the very purpose, even when the consequences do not even occur.[181]

II. Balancing Test

245. After establishing the existence of an unauthorized act, which is a condition for establishing impairment of competition in practice so far, the Agency may, in the rationale of its decisions, also address its effects. Due to the fact that only the operative part of the decision is published on the Agency's website and that no statement of reasons containing detailed arguments is available, it is not possible to see whether the Agency has explained the consequences of impairment of competition in its decisions.

III. Merger Test

246. The Agency shall decide on the approval of the concentration by appraising the effects of concentration on prevention, restriction or distortion of effective competition in the market of Montenegro, and in particular, on creation or strengthening of a dominant position. In this process, the Agency takes into account the following criteria:

(1) the structure and concentration level of the relevant market;
(2) actual and potential competitors;
(3) market position of the parties to the concentration and their economic and financial power;
(4) alternatives available to suppliers and users;
(5) legal and other barriers to entry into the relevant market;
(6) level of internal and international competitiveness of the parties to the concentration;

181. Administrative Court Judgment No. U. 2259/2015, not available online. For detailed explanation of this case, *see* Part II, Ch. 1, §1, I below.

(7) supply and demand trends for the relevant goods and/or services;
(8) trends of technical and economic development; and
(9) the interests of consumers.[182]

247. In practice, in addition to the request for issuance of the approval for implementation of a concentration, the parties to the concentration submit to the Agency, as a part of their notices, the documentation relevant to the determination of the above facts.

248. The Agency has not issued any guidelines on the assessment of the factors listed above. Assessment of concentrations by the Commission is explained in detail in Part II, Chapter 3 below.

182. Competition Act, Art. 54 para. 2.

Chapter 4. Overview of Main Notions

§1. Undertaking

249. The Competition Act applies to legal and natural persons engaged in economic activity and participating in the production of and trade in goods and/or services in the territory of Montenegro.

250. The Competition Act clarifies in detail that its personal scope of the application refers to:

(1) companies and other forms of engaging in an economic activity regardless of their registered office and natural persons regardless of their nationality and residence;
(2) other entities who, directly or indirectly, on a lasting, occasional or one-off basis, engage in economic activity and participate in the trade in goods and/or services, regardless of their nationality, registered office or residence (trade unions, business associations, sports organizations, institutions, cooperatives, intellectual property right holders, etc.); and
(3) public bodies, state administration bodies, local administration bodies and local self-government bodies, when they engage in economic activity directly or indirectly and participate in the trade in goods and/or services.[183]

251. The law defines related undertakings as two or more undertakings connected in such a manner that one undertaking controls another undertaking or more undertakings.[184] The control exists in the case when one undertaking holds in another undertaking: (1) more than half the shares or participating interests, or (2) more than half the voting rights, or (3) the power to appoint more than half the members of the management bodies or persons legally representing the undertaking, or (4) have a decisive influence on management and running of business operations of a company. Related undertakings are deemed to constitute a single undertaking.[185]

§2. Relevant Market

252. The definition of the relevant market is provided in the Competition Act. For the purpose of the Competition Act, the relevant market is the market comprising relevant product market in the relevant geographic market.[186] The criteria for and the method of determination of the relevant market has been prescribed by the Government by Rulebook on criteria for determining the relevant market.

183. Competition Act, Art. 3 para. 1.
184. *Id.*, Art. 4 para. 2.
185. *Id.*, Art. 4 para. 3.
186. *Id.*, Art. 6 para. 1.

I. Relevant Product Market

253. The relevant product market comprises goods and/or services which are regarded as interchangeable or substitutable, by reason of those goods' and services' characteristics, their prices and their intended use.[187] Relevant product market is defined by taking into account particularly price, conditions of procurement, supply, intended use, purchase or sale of products or services deemed to have a very interchangeable character from the aspect of the seller, purchaser/buyer or user.[188]

254. The criteria to be applied for definition of the relevant market shall be the criteria of demand exchangeability of the relevant product or the supply exchangeability by the particular product, depending on the evaluated conditions of competition, the existence and degree of development of potential competition or the obstacles for entering the market.[189] Demand-side exchangeability is a primary test for determining the relevant product market. The demand exchangeability of certain products regarding this Rulebook is the definition of the type and group of products which consumers consider mutually substitutable. The product and the prices do not have to be identical in order to be considered substitutable[190] The possibility of demand exchangeability shall be evaluated on the grounds of available data (submitted and collected during the process), and particularly on the grounds of: (1) general characteristics of goods and services, intended use and quality features; (2) the price of relevant products and complementary products in Montenegro or its part and other, neighbouring markets; (3) amount of material and non-material expenses for the procurement of acceptable substitutive products; (4) long-term sustainability of supply and demand of substitutive products; (5) results of investigations of purchasers, consumers, market participants, conclusions of expert studies and market analyses; (6) possibility of use of the substitutive products in established production and technical-technological system; (7) market dynamics and obstacles for entry, the elasticity of demand, research and development of new products, price correlation, etc.[191] Demand exchangeability shall be additionally evaluated based on the criteria of assessment of the possibility of purchasers and customers to provide appropriate or substitutive products in a relatively short period of time and without significant additional expenses.[192]

255. Supply exchangeability for certain products shall imply the possibility of producers and/or suppliers, in case of the increased price of the relevant products in the short time period and without significant expenses or business risk, to start the production or increase the production and/or distribution of substitutive products and to provide supplies to buyers and consumers on a continuous and long-term base.[193] The possibility of supply exchangeability shall be evaluated on the grounds

187. *Id.*, Art. 6 para. 2.
188. Rulebook on criteria for determining relevant market, Art. 1.
189. *Id.*, Art. 3.
190. *Id.*, Art. 4 para. 1.
191. *Id.*, Art. 4 para. 3.
192. *Id.*, Art. 4 para. 2.
193. *Id.*, Art. 5 para. 1.

of all available data, and it can be particularly evaluated on the grounds of: (1) amount of additional investment and changes of the technical-technological process of production, change of business strategy, investment in the procurement of capital assets of production and turnover; (2) market dynamics, the practice of exchangeability in the previous time period and the research process and development of new products and anticipated influences of development and turnover of the new products to the sale of the relevant products; (3) economic and financial strength of market participants and potential competition; (4) development of production and sale of relevant products and the possibility to increase sales and demand; (5) analyses, studies and opinions of professional public on the possibility of supply exchangeability; (6) application of quantitative tests of elasticity of supply and cross-price elasticity in the previous time period.[194]

II. Relevant Geographic Market

256. Relevant geographic market can be defined depending on exchangeability of demand and supply of products in a shorter time period, and in the absence of significant expenses, as: (1) the territory of Montenegro; (2) geographic area smaller than the territory of Montenegro; or (3) geographic area larger than the territory of Montenegro.[195]

257. If the relevant market is being defined in such a way to cover a geographic area larger or smaller than the area included in administrative borders of the territory of Montenegro, particular attention shall be given to the following facts: (1) purchase power of purchasers or consumers in those areas; (2) the possibility of participants' involvement at the market in those areas regarding the supply of goods or services to purchasers or consumers at the defined relevant geographic market.[196] When determining relevant geographic market outside the territory of Montenegro, particular attention shall be given to the presence of procurement system of the group of purchasers with registered offices in Montenegro who procure relevant products from natural persons or legal entities from the territory of other countries.[197]

258. For the purpose of defining relevant geographic market, the analysis shall be made containing the characteristics of the observed market based on data submitted and collected during the procedure, and particularly on data on market shares of national and international market participants who are considered direct or potential competition, the importance of business at a certain relevant geographic area, the practice of purchase and sale via other geographic markets, a difference of relevant products from other products and services as well as indicators of price and

194. *Id.*, Art. 5 para. 2.
195. *Id.*, Art. 2 para. 2.
196. *Id.*, Art. 2 para. 3.
197. *Id.*, Art. 2 para. 4.

price difference within or outside the territory of Montenegro.[198] Market shares of each undertaking involved in the defined relevant market shall be calculated in accordance with their market shares in production and/or sale of the relevant products in the relevant market in a certain time period. A market share shall be calculated using the value of production and/or sale and/or quantitatively using the quantity of production and/or sale (per unit of measure).[199] In the analysis of characteristics of the observed market, particular attention is given to conditions of market access, and especially to: (1) costs of transport and limitations or road infrastructure; (2) possibility of establishment of distribution channels and access to them and related expenses; (3) presence and influence of regulations defining the market participation (customs, contingents, quotas, regulated prices and conditions of the turnover, licences, public procurement requirements, technical regulations and standards and other similar requirements); (4) habits and practices of consumers, as well as other facts important for determining the degree of market integration of Montenegro with other countries and international organizations.[200]

§3. Market Power/Dominant Position

259. For the definition of dominant position and factors to be used for establishing the existence of market power, *see* Part I, Chapter 3, §2 above.

260. The Competition Act does not cover conduct through which a non-dominant firm becomes or attempts to become dominant. It covers situations of collective dominance *see* Part I, Chapter 3, §2 above.

261. One of the Supreme Court's judgments regarding abuse of a dominant position in the case of Vodovod Budva states the following: There has been an abuse of a dominant position if a business entity with 100% participation in a defined market imposes an unjustifiably high cost of service by directly fixing a special monthly maintenance fee and reading of the water metre as an additional cost.[201]

262. In cases so far, the Agency did not have a difficult task in establishing dominance.

§4. Agreements and Concerted Practices

263. For the definition of restrictive agreements and concerted practices, *see* Part I, Chapter 3, §1 above.

198. *Id.*, Art. 2 para. 5.
199. *Id.*, Art. 7.
200. *Id.*, Art. 2 para. 6.
201. Judgment of the Supreme Court of Montenegro, No. 415/17 of 19 Oct. 2017. For detailed explanation of this case, *see* Part II, Ch. 2, §1, I below.

I. Agreements

264. Restrictive agreements are prohibited and null and void. In practice, decisions of the Agency in each individual case establishing the existence of a restrictive agreement explicitly state that they are prohibited and null and void.

265. The Montenegrin Competition Act has fully transposed conditions for exemptions from the prohibition, which are derived from Article 101, paragraph 3 of the TFEU. In accordance with Article 9 of the Competition Act, restrictive agreements may be exempted from the prohibition if the following conditions are met:

(1) the agreement contributes to improving the production or distribution of goods or services or to promoting technical or economic progress while;
(2) allowing consumers a fair share of the resulting benefit in the relevant market;
(3) impose only restrictions which are indispensable to the attainment of objectives of the agreements; and
(4) do not afford such undertakings the possibility of eliminating competition in the relevant market or a substantial part thereof.[202]

266. An exemption can be granted for a group of agreements or on an individual basis. The agreements fulfilling the conditions prescribed for block exemption do not require the approval by the Agency. Individual exemption must be requested and obtained from the Agency in each individual case.[203]

267. The term *agreement* should be broadly interpreted in practice. For example, even actions that would not be perceived as agreements in civil contract law (gentlemen's agreements) can be interpreted as agreements in light of Article 8 of the Competition Act.

II. Concerted Practices

268. Agreements and decisions are relatively easy to analyse and detect. However, the term concerted practice is not as clear as the previous terms. In fact, concerted practices are one of the most complex concepts in EU competition law.

269. In the EU, one of the very first cases to frame the concept of concerted practices was the *Dyestuffs Case*.[204] It can be observed from this case that dyestuff producers were closely cooperating in the common market while making similar price increases at the same time. During the period 1964–1967, manufacturers from different countries made various price announcements while similarly increasing

202. Competition Act, Art. 9.
203. *Id.*, Art. 12.
204. *Imperial Chemical Industries Ltd v. Commission of the European communities*, Case No. 48-69 (14 Jul. 1972).

their prices for dyestuffs three different times, and almost at the same time. Moreover, a meeting was organized before the last price increase in 1967, and it was attended by these producers who reported their prices to the competitors. It was concluded by the Commission that these price announcements between the dyestuff producers were an example of concerted practice.

270. By a decision of 31 May 1967, the Commission commenced proceedings under Article 3 of Regulation No. 17/62 concerning these increases for presumed infringement of Article 85(1) of the European Economic Community treaty against seventeen producers of dyestuffs established within and outside the common market and against numerous subsidiaries and representatives of those undertakings. It demonstrated that the price increases were in relation to the same products and at similar rates. When the case came before the CJEU, the Advocate General stated the differences between concerted practice and agreement in his opinion. He stressed that concerted practice must *have effects on competition in the market, but on the other side, agreements can only have objects, which do not need to be proven to have any effects on the market.*

271. The Agency did not establish an impairment of competition in the form of a concerted practice.

§5. Restriction of Competition

272. Article 7 of the Competition Act contains a general prohibition of anticompetitive conduct. For the purpose of the Competition Act, the acts (in Montenegrin: *akti*) or practices (In Montengrin: *radnje*) impairing competition in the market are as follows:

(1) agreements preventing, restricting or distorting competition (restrictive agreements);
(2) abuse of dominant position; and
(3) concentrations preventing, restricting or distorting competition or free development of open market economy, and in particular, creation and/or strengthening of a dominant position in the market.[205]

§6. Monopolization and Abuse of Dominance

273. The definition of abuse of dominance has been fully transposed in Montenegrin competition law from Article 102 of the TFEU. The abuse of dominance exists in the following cases:

205. Competition Act, Art. 7.

(1) directly or indirectly imposing unfair purchase or selling prices or other unfair trading conditions;
(2) limiting production, markets or technical development to the prejudice of consumers;
(3) applying dissimilar conditions to equivalent transactions with other undertakings, thereby placing them at a competitive disadvantage;
(4) making the conclusion of contracts subject to acceptance of supplementary obligations which, by their nature or according to commercial usage, have no connection with the subject of such contracts.[206]

274. The Competition Act does not contain the notion of *monopolization.*

§7. CONCENTRATIONS

275. As elaborated in Part I, Chapter 3, §3 above, concentration in accordance with the Competition Act has arisen in three forms: (i) merger, (ii) acquisition and (iii) joint venture.

276. Concentration in the form of merger exists in case of one of the types of status changes regulated by the Company Act: (1) by merger; (2) by division into two or more separate companies; (3) by carving out a portion of the company's assets to constitute one or more companies (spin-off). A merger happens in the following cases: (i) when one or more companies join the existing company by transferring the entire assets and liabilities to that company which in exchange issues shares to the shareholders of the companies being merged; or (ii) two or more companies merge into a newly-formed company that issues shares of the newly-formed company to the shareholders of the companies being merged.[207] A joint-stock company shall cease to exist by restructuring by way of division, by entirely transferring its assets and liabilities to two or more existing or newly-formed companies, which will in exchange issue shares that are distributed to shareholders of the dividing company.[208] By spin-off, the existing company shall transfer a part of its assets and liabilities to one or more companies that are established (new company), which will in exchange issue shares that are distributed to the shareholders of the existing company whose capital is reduced by the value of the transferred assets.[209]

277. The second situation in which a concentration could arise involves a change of control over an undertaking. As explained earlier, the control exists in the case when one undertaking holds in another undertaking: (1) more than half the shares or participating interests, or more than half the voting rights, or (2) have the power to appoint more than half the members of the management bodies or persons

206. *Id.*, Art. 15.
207. Company Act, Art. 22a para. 1.
208. *Id.*, Art. 22v para. 1.
209. *Id.*, Art. 22g para. 1.

legally representing the undertaking, or (3) have a decisive influence on management and running of business operations of a company.

278. Two or more transactions between the same undertakings which take place within a two-year period are treated as one and the same concentration.[210]

§8. Joint Ventures

279. In Montenegrin competition law regulation, a joint venture can be examined in the context of merger control or under the provisions on restrictive agreements.

280. Joint ventures fall under concentration in a situation when two or more independent undertakings establish a new undertaking or acquire joint control of the existing undertaking which operates independently on a lasting basis and performs all the functions of an autonomous undertaking.[211]

281. To fall under the provision of the mentioned Article 16 of the Competition Act which deals with concentrations, the created joint venture undertaking must perform, on a lasting basis, all the functions of an autonomous economic entity. For example, the existence of a separate staff and management structure of the joint venture is a precondition. A full-function joint venture cannot be established in cases where the joint venture performs solely one specific function within the parent companies' business activities without access to the market.

282. When a joint venture has been made with the object of coordination of market activities between two or more undertakings that remain legally independent, it shall not be deemed as concentration. In such a situation, joint ventures will be appraised as a restrictive agreement in accordance with Article 9 of the Competition Act.

283. In the process of assessing whether a joint venture falls under the regime of concentration or can be assessed as restrictive agreement, the Agency relies on EU sources, especially to Council Regulation (EC) No. 139/2004 of 20 January 2004 on the control of concentrations between undertakings.[212]

---

210. Competition Act, Art. 16 para. 4.
211. *Id.*, Art. 16 para. 1 item 3.
212. O.J [2008] C 95/1.

Chapter 5. Consequences of Violations and Enforcement Institutions

§1. Administrative Enforcement

I. The Antitrust Authorities

284. The Agency is the only authority in Montenegro with the sole competence to enforce competition laws and regulations. However, as mentioned before, certain regulators in specific sectors have also powers in relation to competition law regulation in Montenegro.[213]

285. As explained in the earlier text, the Agency as an independent body was established in 2012. The Agency started working on the day of registration in the Central Registry of Business Entities of the Tax Administration (8 February 2013). Lack of efficiency in the work of the previous competition authority and, above all, its position in public administration as an organizational unit within the Ministry of economy, puts pressure to Montenegrin authorities to give more independence to state body responsible for the competition, and finally led to changes in 2012. By the last amendment of the Competition Act in 2018, its powers and jurisdiction were significantly expanded.

286. At the beginning of work, the powers were limited as it lacked the independence of being an office within the ministry. Also, it has a problem with staff and especially professionals with deeper knowledge regarding competition law. Gradually, over time, things have changed in terms of hiring professional staff and the volume of work of the Agency. However, this Agency is under constant pressure from the overall public. By inspecting the Annual Reports of the Agency, it can be concluded that the number of employees and the volume of activities gradually increased from 2012.

287. The Agency has its own Statute which regulates internal organization and manner of business, detailed powers and scope of work of the bodies of the Agency, the manner of and procedure for decision-making, adoption and publication of general acts and other issues relevant to the work of the Agency. The Agency is authorized to enact its own by-laws and to regulate the internal organization in detail. The Government of Montenegro gives consent to the Statute of the Agency. Based on the Statute, the Agency's Code of Ethics was adopted in June 2013. The Code of Ethics governs the rules of conduct and ethical standards of employees.

---

213. *See* Part I, Ch. 2, §2 above.

A. Formation, Composition

288. The Competition Act prescribes as general principle independence of the Agency, its management bodies and all staff. However, the Agency does not have financial independence. Funds for financing the Agency are provided from the Budget of Montenegro. The Agency's financial plan is subject to prior approval by the Ministry of Finance and the Government of Montenegro. The Agency is obliged to prepare and publish its activity report for the preceding year and the annual financial statement, including the auditor's report on its website.[214] The Agency is accountable for its work to the Government.[215] The seat of the Agency is in Podgorica.

289. In accordance with the Competition Act, the Agency has the following competence in the area of competition to:

(1) monitor and analyse conditions of competition in the general market as well as in the markets of particular economic sectors;[216]
(2) define research methods for competition;[217]
(3) approve exemptions from the prohibition of certain agreements and approve concentrations of undertakings, under prescribed conditions and take decisions in other matters in accordance with the Competition Act;[218]
(4) take measures against undertakings and associations of undertakings for impairment of competition in the market, or take measures with a view to preventing the occurrence of or terminating the infringement and eliminating harmful effects for undertakings and consumers;[219]
(5) conduct administrative procedure and take decisions in individual administrative matters;[220]
(6) file request for initiating misdemeanour proceedings to the competent authority and/or issue misdemeanour orders in accordance with the law that regulates misdemeanours;[221]
(7) give opinions regarding applicable legislation that affect or may affect competition and inform the public thereof;[222]
(8) cooperate with international and national organizations and institutions in the field of competition;[223]
(9) publish statistical data and keep records of approved and notified concentrations.[224]

214. Competition Act, Art. 19 para. 3.
215. *Id.*, Art. 20 para. 1.
216. *Id.*, Art. 20 para. 2 item 1.
217. *Id.*, Art. 20 para. 2 item 2.
218. *Id.*, Art. 20 para. 2 item 3.
219. *Id.*, Art. 20 para. 2 item 4.
220. *Id.*, Art. 20 para. 2 item 19.
221. *Id.*, Art. 20 para. 2 item 20.
222. *Id.*, Art. 20 para. 2 item 21.
223. *Id.*, Art. 20 para. 2 item 23.
224. *Id.*, Art. 20 para. 2 item 26.

290. According to last amendments of the Competition Act in 2018, the bodies of the Agency are the Council and the Director of the Agency.[225]

291. The Council has a President and two members. The President and one member of the Council are appointed by the Government on a proposal from the Ministry, while the other member of the Council shall be appointed by the Government on a proposal from the state administration body competent for State aid. The President and members of the Council are appointed for a period of four years and may be reappointed. They exercise their offices in the Agency on a professional basis. Also, they may not be a Member of the Parliament or another public office or perform another activity on a professional basis.[226]

292. The Council has competence for the adoption of normative acts and the work report of the Agency for the preceding year; the annual work plan in the field of State aid and the annual report on the granted State aid. Normative activities of the Council include the adoption of the following acts: (i) administrative acts falling within the competence of the Agency;[227] (ii) the rules of the Agency;[228] (iii) the Rules of Operation of the Council;[229] (iv) the statute and the act on internal organization and systematization of work posts; and (v) other acts of the Agency.[230] Also, the Council has the competence to give opinions and guidelines on the application of legislation related to the protection of competition and State aid.[231]

293. The Council submits to the Government the proposed financial plan of the Agency for the following year.

294. The Council takes decisions by a majority vote of the total number of members. Convening the meetings of the Council, manner of decision-making and other matters relevant to the work of the Council has been regulated by the statute of the Agency.[232]

295. The President of the Council presides at the meetings of the Council, signs decisions and other acts of the Council, proposes measures to improve the work of the Council and performs other tasks laid down in the Competition Act and the statute of the Agency.[233]

296. The President and the Council members may be elected among experts in the field of law and economics. The Competition Act prescribes three conditions for the election of the President and the Council members: (i) Montenegrin nationality;

225. *Id.*, Art. 20a.
226. *Id.*, Art. 20b.
227. *Id.*, Art. 20f para. 1 item 1.
228. *Id.*, Art. 20f para. 1 item 2.
229. *Id.*, Art. 20f para. 1 item 3.
230. *Id.*, Art. 20f para. 1 item 4.
231. *Id.*, Art. 20f para. 1 item 8.
232. *Id.*, Art. 20g.
233. *Id.*, Art. 20h.

(ii) to hold at least VII-1 level of educational qualification in the field of law or economics; (iii) to have at least five years of work experience in the field of protection of competition and state aid.[234]

297. The Competition Act sets restrictions on the Election of the President and Members of the Council. A person may not be appointed as a President or a member of the Council if: (1) he is a Member of the Parliament or a councillor; (2) he is a member of the Government; (3) he has been appointed by the President of Montenegro, the Parliament, the Government or an assembly of the local self-government; (4) he is an official of a political party (president of a party, member of a presidency, his deputy, member of the executive and main board, and other party officials); (5) he has been finally convicted of criminal offence prosecuted ex officio, regardless of the sanction imposed, or if he has been finally convicted of other criminal offence and sentenced to a prison term longer than six months, in the period while the legal consequences of the conviction last; and (6) he is a relative of the person referred to in items 1–4 in the straight line or in the collateral line up to the second degree of kinship, a relative by marriage up to the first degree of kinship, a married or a common-law spouse, adoptive parent or adoptee, and a member of his joint household.[235] A candidate for a member of the Council shall submit to the competent body of the Government a written statement that there are no impediments to appointment set out in the Competition Act.[236]

298. The President and/or a member of the Council may be dismissed before the expiry of the period of his appointment: (1) on his personal request; (2) if he permanently loses the working capacity to exercise his office; (3) in case of occurrence of the restrictions on the election of the President and Members of the Council; (4) if he discharges the duty of the President or a member of the Council untimely and unconscientiously; (5) if he provides inaccurate data in the written statement that there are no impediments to the appointment.[237]

299. According to the Competition Act, as amended in 2018, the Agency is managed by the Director of the Agency. The Director of the Agency is appointed by the Government on a proposal from the Ministry.[238] The Director of the Agency has a deputy and two assistants – one assistant for the protection of competition and one assistant for State aid. The Deputy Director of the Agency is appointed by the Government on a proposal from the Ministry of Economy, and Assistant Director of the Agency is appointed by the Government on a proposal from the Director of the Agency.[239]

300. The Director of the Agency shall have the power to: (1) act on behalf of and represent the Agency; (2) be responsible for the legality of operation of the

234. *Id.*, Art. 20c.
235. *Id.*, Art. 20d.
236. *Id.*, Art. 20d para. 2.
237. *Id.*, Art. 20e.
238. *Id.*, Art. 21 paras 1, 2.
239. *Id.*, Art. 21 paras 3, 4, 5.

Agency; (3) organize and manage operations of the Agency; (4) propose to the Council administrative acts within the competence of the Agency and take care of the execution of the Council's decisions; (5) propose to the Council activity report for the preceding year and a financial plan for each subsequent year; (6) submit to the Council a proposal of opinion on the application of regulations in the field of competition and state aid; (7) file request for initiating misdemeanour proceedings to the competent authority and/or issue misdemeanour orders; (8) decide on the rights, obligations and responsibilities of employees of the Agency; (9) make decisions on the revenue and expenditure management of the Agency in accordance with the financial plan.[240]

301. The Director of the Agency and the Council members enjoy the status of a functionary within the meaning of the law governing conflict of interest in the performance of public duty.[241]

302. The President and members of the Council of the Agency, the Director of the Agency and the employees of the Agency may not seek or receive guidance from state bodies, local self-government bodies, legal entities and other entities exercising public authority or other legal and natural persons in performing the activities and duties determined by the Competition Act.[242]

303. The Rulebook on internal organization and job classification of workplaces in Agency (in Montenegrin: *Pravilnik o unutrašnjoj organizaciji i klasifikaciji poslova u Agenciji*) has divided activities within the two organizational units: the sector for concentration assessment, the establishment of prohibited agreements and abuse of dominant position and the general affairs and finance service. The competencies of the sector are divided into three sections as follows: (i) Department for the protection of competition in regulated markets in the electronics sector communication, information technologies and the media; (ii) Department for the protection of competition of the financial market, healthcare, free professions and other services; (iii) Department for the protection of competition in the energy, construction, forestry, mining, tourism, transport, agriculture and chemical products.[243]

304. The Agency lacks a significant number of employees in order to improve its efficiency. Unlike sectoral regulators (who control and regulate business in only one business sector), which usually have a large number of employees, there are twelve employees in the Agency. Out of this number, five persons were employed in 2017.[244]

---

240. *Id.*, Art. 22.
241. Law on Prevention of Corruption (*Zakon o sprječavanju korupcije, Službeni list Crne Gore,* 053/14 and 042/17).
242. Competition Act, Art. 19 para. 4.
243. The Rulebook on Internal Organisation and Job Classification of Workplaces (*Pravilnik o unutrašnjoj organizaciji i sistematizaciji radnih mjesta*).
244. Agency's Annual Report for 2017, p. 27.

305. Regulations regulating the position and salaries of civil servants and state employees are applied to the rights and obligations of employees in the Agency.[245]

306. The Agency is financed in accordance with a financial plan which the Agency adopts on an annual basis and submits to the Government for approval no later than by 1 November of a current year for the next year.[246]

307. The Competition Act prescribes that resources necessary for the operation of the Agency shall be provided from: (1) the fees paid to the Agency in accordance with the Competition Act; (2) the budget of Montenegro; (3) donations; and (4) other sources in accordance with the law.[247] The fees paid to the Agency have been determined by Tariff on the amount of fees payable in the procedure before the Competition Agency adopted by the Agency, with the previous consent of the Government.[248] The amount of fees are determined for acts issued by the Agency to individual market participants. The proposed solutions in the Tariff allow the interested market participants to, before submitting a request to the Agency, be informed of the level of fees that it will be responsible for issuing documents by the Agency at their request. Fees are recorded and found on a separate account with the CBM. At the end of the calendar year, the total amount of funds realized on this basis is transferred to the Budget of Montenegro.

308. The annual financial statement of the Agency is subject to an annual audit by an independent certified auditor. The Agency is obliged to submit the annual financial statement with auditor's report to the Government by the end of the second quarter of the current year.[249]

309. Finally, regarding financial independence, it can be concluded that the Agency does not have financial independence, it does not have its account, and it is financed from the Budget of Montenegro.

B. Investigation Powers

310. In the proceedings for examining the existence of a prohibited agreement, the abuse of a dominant position or the assessment of the permissibility of carrying out a concentration, the Agency acts in compliance with the general regulations in force for all bodies with entrusted public authority in Montenegro. In this sense, in addition to regulations and powers from other laws on conducting administrative proceedings, the procedural rules are contained in the Competition Act itself with

245. Law on Salaries in Public Sector (*Zakon o zaradama zaposlenih u javnom sektoru, Službeni list Crne Gore* 16/2016, 42/2017 and 39/2018).
246. Competition Act, Art. 25 para. 1.
247. *Id.*, Art. 24 para. 1.
248. *Tarifnik o visini naknada koje se plaćaju u postupku pred Agencijom za zaštitu konkurencije, Službeni list Crne Gore* 14/13.
249. Competition Act, Art. 25 paras 6 and 7.

the aim of ensuring full and adequate application of the provisions of Council Regulation (EC) No. 1/2003.[250] The aforementioned decision is especially evident in the authority of the Agency to carry out a dawn raid, collect evidence during the proceedings and exchange information with other state authorities and non-party business entities.

311. The Agency was given considerable powers by the Competition Act. During the process of establishing impairment of competition, the Agency may take statements from parties, witnesses, perform expert witnesses, obtain data, documents and things, collect data through direct access and temporarily seize things.[251] Throughout the proceedings, the Agency may take statements from any person who may have direct and indirect knowledge of the infringement of competition law. In practice, the primary source of information and facts for the Agency is collected through requests for information and documentation. Pursuant to Article 18 EU Regulation No. 1/2003, the Competition Act provides for an obligation for all market participants to submit, under the Agency's order, all required data and documentation within fifteen days, under threat of sanction.[252] A sanction is also provided for in cases where incomplete or untrue information is provided, while any decision may be overturned and proceedings re-opened if it is based on incomplete, false or inaccurate information.

312. For a more detailed explanation of the Agency's investigation powers, *see* Part III, Chapter 1, §2, II below.

C. Adjudication Powers (Asserting and Sanctioning)

313. The main adjudicating power of the Agency is to establish infringement of competition.

314. Also, in accordance with the Competition Act, the Agency has the power to grant individual exemptions from prohibition and to clear (conditionally or unconditionally) or prohibit a concentration.

315. With regard to the imposition of a sanction, it is important to emphasize that the Agency does not have the authority to impose sanctions for the impairment of competition. This decision has been rightly criticized by competition law experts and in the European Commission's Annual Reports. Hence, the sanctions for impairment of competition, provided for by the Competition Act, are imposed by the competent misdemeanour court. In the Agency's 2017 Report, it was pointed out that

---

250. Council Regulation (EC) No. 1/2003 of 16 Dec. 2002 on the implementation of the rules on competition laid down in Arts 81 and 82 of the Treaty. O.J. [2003] L 0011.
251. Competition Act, Art. 31.
252. *Id.*, Art. 39.

since the Competition Act came into force, the competent misdemeanour courts had imposed only two sentences for the violation of competition.[253]

316. The Agency has the authority to determine periodic fines during the process of establishing competition violations when collecting information, data and documentation. The Agency may also order structural and/or behavioural measures by a decision on the impairment of competition. These forms of sanctioning will be explained below in detail.

D. Other Institutional Tasks (Consultancy to Parliament/Government)

317. In accordance with the Competition Act, the Agency gives opinions regarding applicable legislation that affect or may affect competition.[254] Also, the Agency gives an opinion on the application of regulations in the field of competition protection.[255] This is especially evident through communication and cooperation with sectoral regulators.

II. Government Direct Enforcement Activities

318. The Government does not have the power to directly enforce the competition law. Nevertheless, the Government plays an important role in creating the competition policy through its power to create an overall business environment and enact decrees in the areas of protection of competition.

III. Other Administrative Agencies Applying Antitrust Rules

319. On special administrative agencies with powers to regulate and enforce antitrust-related matters, *see* Part I, Chapter 2, §2 above.

IV. Administrative Fines

A. Types of Fines and Procedure for Imposition

320. The Competition Act defines different types of fines: (i) fines in the percentage of total turnover in the previous accounting year imposed for misdemeanours in cases of impairment of competition; (ii) periodic fines imposed for violation of the procedure before the Agency.

253. Agency's Annual Report for 2017, pp. 74–75.
254. Competition Act, Art. 19 para. 1 item 21.
255. *Id.*, Art. 19 para. 1 item 16.

321. According to the existing legal solution in Montenegro, the Agency is not authorized to impose fines for misdemeanours (the only exemption is minimal penalties imposed by misdemeanour order). The right to impose misdemeanours penalties is within the competence of the Misdemeanour Courts and its departments on the territory of Montenegro. The Law on Misdemeanours regulates the standards for determining misdemeanours and misdemeanour sanctions, misdemeanour liability, misdemeanour proceedings, and the procedure for the enforcement of misdemeanour sanctions.[256] The Agency has the power to impose procedural penalties which are regulated by the Competition Act.

322. This legal solution is applicable to all other sectoral regulators who have the power to monitor the market in accordance with special laws.

323. Thus, in Montenegrin law, misdemeanour courts have the exclusive right to impose misdemeanour sanctions, while the role of regulators is to initiate misdemeanour proceedings. However, in practice, there are often problems with sanctioning. First, employees in special agencies tend to have more expertise than misdemeanour court judges because they only deal with specific sectors. In contrast, misdemeanour court judges deal with misdemeanour law in various fields and consequently lack sufficient professional experience in interpreting the challenging rules of competition law. Second, in practice, because of the above, the very essence of decision-making is neglected, but the emphasis is often on compliance with the appropriate procedure as the outcome of the proceedings depends on this compliance.

324. It is important to emphasize that in practice so far, the Agency has changed its practice when it comes to the time of initiating misdemeanour proceedings. In the first cases, the Agency waited for the proceedings for establishing impairment of competition to be finalized, and after that, it initiated misdemeanour proceedings. The aforementioned practice resulted in the fact that the statute of limitations occurred in certain misdemeanour proceedings. Due to the above, in recent years, the practice of the Agency is to initiate misdemeanour proceedings before the competent court after issuing a decision to initiate the proceedings for establishing impairment of competition. Therefore, it is often the case that the administrative procedure for establishing impairment of competition before the Agency, and the misdemeanour proceedings before the competent misdemeanour court are conducted at the same time.

325. The Agency has the possibility to issue misdemeanour order where a violation of competition law has been found. However, the Agency may impose the minimum prescribed fine in the misdemeanour order. Misdemeanour Act prescribes that an authorized body shall issue a misdemeanour order if it is determined in any

256. Law on Misdemeanours (*Zakon o prekršajima, Službeni list Crne Gore* 001/11, 032/14, 051/17).

of the following ways: (1) direct observation of an authorized officer while conducting an inspection, supervision or review, as well as while performing an inspection of the official records of a competent body;[257] (2) on the basis of information obtained by means of supervision or measurement devices;[258] (3) in the course inspecting documentation, premises and goods or through other legal means;[259] (4) on the basis of the accused person's admission that he committed the misdemeanour, given before an authorized body at the scene or at another court or administrative proceeding.[260] The accused may accept responsibility for a misdemeanour by paying the fine and fulfilling all other obligations set forth in the misdemeanour order within the specified deadline, or by notifying the authorized body that he accepts the sanction set forth in the misdemeanour order.[261] If the accused who has been issued a misdemeanour order does not assume misdemeanour liability, he/she may submit to the competent court, in person, through another person or by post, a Petition for Court Adjudication with all the available evidence, within eight days from the day of serving the order.

326. In accordance with Law on Misdemeanours, misdemeanour proceedings may be initiated on the basis of: (1) a petition for court adjudication of the misdemeanour order which is submitted in the original, or (2) a petition to initiate misdemeanour proceedings.[262] In practice, in case of non-acceptance of the imposed fine by administrative order, the Misdemeanour Court decides based on a petition for court adjudication of the misdemeanour order.

327. First instance misdemeanour proceedings shall be presided over by a single judge. The second instance court shall adjudicate in a three-judge panel.[263] Misdemeanour proceedings shall end with the rendering of a decision acquitting the defendant, a decision finding the defendant guilty, or a decision dismissing the misdemeanour proceedings.[264]

328. Against decisions rendered in the first instance of misdemeanour courts, an appeal may be filed to the Higher Misdemeanour Court of Montenegro.[265] A timely filed appeal stays the execution of the judicial decision.[266] At the session of the Panel, the second instance court may: (1) dismiss an appeal as belated or as inadmissible; (2) reject an appeal as unfounded and reaffirm the decision of the first instance court; (3) revoke the first instance decision and remand the case to the first instance court for de novo adjudication; (4) reverse the first instance decision.[267]

---

257. *Id.*, Art. 144 para. 1 item 1.
258. *Id.*, Art. 144 para. 1 item 2.
259. *Id.*, Art. 144 para. 1 item 3.
260. *Id.*, Art. 144 para. 1 item 3.
261. *Id.*, Art. 147 para. 1.
262. *Id.*, Art. 143.
263. *Id.*, Art. 107.
264. *Id.*, Art. 193 para. 1.
265. *Id.*, Art. 105.
266. *Id.*, Art. 199 para. 2.
267. *Id.*

329. For example, in the Montenegrin public significant attention was drawn to the misdemeanour proceedings against the company Vodovod i Kanalizacija DOO Budva.[268] The Misdemeanour Court in Budva found this company and its responsible person guilty, following the proceedings, and imposed a fine amounting to EUR 61,553.00 for the legal entity, or EUR 1,000 for the responsible person in the legal entity.[269] The High Misdemeanour Court rejected as unfounded the appeal of the defendants and upheld the first instance decision of the Misdemeanour Court.[270] So far, this is the highest penalty in misdemeanour proceedings in cases of protection of competition. The High Misdemeanour Court ruled in the same manner in the case against the company Urion Podgorica and its responsible person.[271] In the first instance proceedings before the Misdemeanour Court in Podgorica, the company Urion Podgorica and its responsible person were found guilty and fined.[272]

330. In the Montemedicon case, the High Court upheld the Agency's appeal, quashed the first instance decision of the Misdemeanour Court, and remitted the case to that court for reconsideration.[273] In the present case, by a first instance decision of the Misdemeanour Court in Podgorica, the company Montemedicom and the responsible person in this company were acquitted of misdemeanour liability for violation of competition law.[274]

331. In practice, there are also cases where the High Misdemeanour Court modified decisions of the First Instance Misdemeanour Court. However, this is not a common practice. For example, in the proceedings initiated by the Agency against Luka Kotor and its executive director, the High Misdemeanour Court in Budva in its first instance decision exonerated these persons of the responsibility due to the lack of evidence. However, the High Misdemeanour Court upheld the Agency's appeal and reversed the decision of the Misdemeanour Court in Budva by holding Luka Kotor and its executive director responsible for violating competition law (abuse of a dominant position) and imposing appropriate misdemeanour sanctions against them.[275]

332. The Agency has the possibility to continue the procedure through The Supreme State Prosecutor's Office. The Supreme State Prosecutor's Office may file

268. Proceedings before the Agency for impairment of competition will be detailed explained in the text below. *See* Part II, Ch. 2, §1, I below.
269. Decision No. PP. 163/17 of 20 Nov. 2017, not available online.
270. Decision No. PŽP. 1810/17-2 of 28 Dec. 2017, not available online.
271. Decision No. PŽP. 192/18-17 of 26 Mar. 2018, not available online.
272. Decision No. PP. 3671/16-26 of 20 Dec. 2017, not available online. Proceedings before the Agency for impairment of competition will be detailed explained in the text below. *See* Part II, Ch. 1, §1, I below.
273. Decision No. PŽP. 1731/17-3 of 28 Dec. 2017, not available online.
274. Decision No. PP. 3672/16-21 of 4 Jul. 2017, not available online. Proceedings before the Agency for impairment of competition will be detailed explained in the text below. *See* Part II, Ch. 1, §1, I below.
275. Decision No. PŽP. 920/18-6 of 10 Jul. 2018, not available online. Proceedings before the Agency for impairment of competition will be detailed explained in the text below. *See* Part II, Ch. 2, §2, IV below.

a request for protection of legality against final judicial decisions if a law or some other piece of legislation have been violated.[276] Supreme Court of Montenegro is authorized to decide on the request for protection of legality.

333. In this proceedings, the Supreme Court decides in a panel of three judges.[277] When deciding on a petition for protection of legality, the Supreme Court is limited only to examining violations of law or other regulation from the petition of the Supreme State Prosecutor's Office.[278] The Supreme Court shall reject a petition for protection of legality as unfounded if it finds that there is no violation of the law or other regulation referred to in the petition.[279] When the Supreme Court determines that the petition for protection of legality is well-founded, it may make one of the following decisions: (i) reverse the final decision, (ii) entirely or partly quash the first instance and second instance decision and remand the case to the first instance court for reconsideration; or (iii) shall confine itself only to the determination of whether there has been a violation of the law or other piece of legislation.[280]

334. The Competition Act prescribes the following misdemeanours which can be executed if undertaking: (1) negotiates the conclusion of, concludes or enforces a restrictive agreement;[281] (2) abuses its dominant position on the market;[282] (3) implements prohibited concentration;[283] (4) does not suspend implementation of concentration until the Agency adopts decision approving intended concentration;[284] (5) does not comply, fully or partially, with the measures, conditions and time limits imposed by the decision of the Agency in specific cases.[285]

335. The maximum amount of fine that can be imposed is 10% aggregate annual turnover in the financial year preceding the year in which a misdemeanour was committed. The Competition Act does not specify does it norms apply to annual turnover gained in Montenegrin market or the overall market. It can be concluded that the wording of the norm allows the Agency to calculate the amount of the fine based on the infringer's worldwide turnover.

336. Also, a fine in the amount from EUR 1,000 to EUR 4,000 can be imposed on the responsible person in an undertaking, as well as on the responsible person in

---

276. Misdemeanour Act, Art. 224 para. 1.
277. *Id.*, Art. 224a para. 1.
278. *Id.*, Art. 224b para. 1.
279. *Id.*, Art. 224b para. 2.
280. *Id.*, Art. 224b para. 3.
281. Competition Act, Art. 67 para. 1 item 1.
282. *Id.*, Art. 67 para. 1 item 2.
283. *Id.*, Art. 67 para. 1 item 3.
284. *Id.*, Art. 67 para. 1 item 4.
285. *Id.*, Art. 67 para. 1 item 5.

a public body, state administration body, local administration body and local self-government body, if such body acts as an undertaking, for above misdemeanours.[286]

337. Finally, in a separate article, the Competition Act has introduced a fine to undertaking who fails to submit the request for issuance of the approval for implementation of a concentration within the specified period. A fine can be determined in the amount from EUR 4,000 to EUR 40,000.[287] A fine in the amount from EUR 1,000 to EUR 4,000 shall also be imposed on the responsible person.[288]

338. The Law on Misdemeanours provides that for the most serious misdemeanours in the areas of prevention, restriction or distortion of competition, the amount of the fine may be prescribed at the percentage of 1%–10% of the total annual revenue of the undertakings, for the fiscal year which preceded the year in which the misdemeanour was committed.[289] In a Misdemeanour Decision, the period of payment of a fine shall be specified, which may not be less than eight days, nor longer than sixty days from the date the Misdemeanour Decision becomes final and enforceable. In justified cases (depending on the amount of the fine and the material situation of the defendant), the court may order payment of the imposed fine in instalments, but the instalments must be paid over a length of time that does not exceed six months.[290] An imposed penalty cannot be enforced if two years have passed from the date the Misdemeanour Decision became final and legally binding, and enforceable.[291]

339. Proceeds gained from the payment of fines imposed for the commission of a misdemeanour are considered part of the state budget revenue, except for proceeds gained from fines for misdemeanours that are violations of laws whose application is the responsibility of a local administrative body, in which case such proceeds are part of the revenue of that local administrative body.[292]

340. The proceedings for establishing impairment of competition may not be initiated if two years elapse from the day when the misdemeanour was committed.[293] Prosecution shall become barred by lapse of time in any case when four years elapse from the day when the misdemeanour was committed.[294]

341. The Agency is entitled to impose procedural monetary penalties, if an undertaking: (1) fails to comply with the request of the Agency to supply or communicate required data or if it supplies or communicates incorrect, incomplete or

286. *Id.*, Art. 67 para. 2.
287. *Id.*, Art. 68 para. 1.
288. *Id.*, Art. 68 para. 2.
289. Misdemeanour Act, Art. 24 para. 8.
290. *Id.*, Art. 25.
291. *Id.*, Art. 60 para. 1.
292. *Id.*, Art. 7.
293. Competition Act, Art. 70 para. 1.
294. *Id.*, Art. 70 para. 2.

false information;[295] (2) does not comply with an interim measure ordered by the Agency;[296] (3) designates data or documentation as privileged communication in contravention of Competition Law;[297] (4) the authorized persons or employees obstruct or otherwise prevent the authorized persons of the Agency from undertaking actions of collecting information through inspection of business premises.[298]

342. Procedural penalty can be determined in an amount that ranges between EUR 500 and EUR 5,000 per each day of the breach, provided that the maximum amount of procedural penalty does not exceed 3% of the undertaking's annual turnover in the year preceding the year in which the proceedings were initiated.[299] The time limit for starting to pay the periodic fine may not be longer than fifteen days from the day of receipt of conclusion determining the periodic fine.[300]

343. The Agency determines the amount of the fine and the payment deadline in each individual case.

B. Leniency

344. Montenegrin legal system has leniency institute, which can be applicable under certain conditions prescribed by the Competition Act. This institute allows a party to a restrictive agreement to be excluded from fine or a reduction of fine. More precisely, the Agency may decide: (1) not to submit the request for initiating misdemeanour proceedings; (2) to withdraw the request already submitted or (3) to propose to the court during the proceedings more lenient punishment of the party.[301] Also, the Agency may, applying analogously to the law regulating misdemeanour proceedings, propose to the party to the restrictive agreement to conclude the agreement on the admission of guilt.[302]

345. Leniency is available to horizontal cartels, vertical and combined horizontal-vertical restrictive agreements. However, leniency is not applicable to a party who initiated or organized conclusion or enforcement of the restrictive agreement.[303] Also, leniency is not possible for abuse of dominance.

346. A party to a restrictive agreement may be granted immunity from fine, under fulfilment of the following requirement:

295. *Id.*, Art. 60 para. 1 item 1.
296. *Id.*, Art. 60 para. 1 item 2.
297. *Id.*, Art. 60 para. 1 item 3.
298. *Id.*, Art. 60 para. 1 item 4.
299. *Id.*, 60 para. 1.
300. *Id.*, Art. 60 para. 3.
301. *Id.*, Art. 69 para. 1.
302. *Id.*, Art. 69 para. 3.
303. *Id.*, Art. 69 para. 2.

(1) is the first to report to the Agency the existence of the agreement and submits valid evidence;[304]
(2) submits evidence of the existence of the restrictive agreement to the Agency which at that moment had some knowledge thereof but did not have sufficient evidence;[305]
(3) reports existence of another prohibited agreement it is a party to or has immediate knowledge of, of which it has supplied evidence.[306]

347. In the previous practice, the Agency had only one application on this basis, in the already initiated procedure, when the implementation of this institute for the Agency had no significance, especially when they were already there was clear evidence and evidence in possession of the Agency.

V. Administrative Injunctions and Other Restrictive Orders

A. *In the Course of Investigation*

348. The Competition Act gives power to the Agency to conduct an effective investigation. In the investigation procedure, the Agency is, *inter alia*, authorized to issue certain injunctions and restrictive orders.[307]

349. During investigation procedure, the Agency may order temporarily seizing of documents, objects or devices. The investigation is conducted by the authorized persons of the Agency designated by the Director of the Agency on a case-by-case basis. Procedural order of temporary seizure of documents or objects is rendered usually by this person. Temporary seized documents or objects are kept by the Agency until extraction of all relevant facts and information. However, the Competition Act does not regulate in detail the procedure in this situation. A conclusion on taking evidence is not subject to a separate appeal and can be challenged only in the challenge of the final decision.

350. The authorized persons of the Agency are obliged to record all documents, materials and other items subject to inspection and seizure, and deliver a copy of the record to the person whose premises have been searched.

B. *Following the Finding of Infringement*

351. By the decision establishing the impairment of competition, the Agency may order the infringer to implement appropriate behavioural or structural measures.

---

304. *Id.*, Art. 69 para. 1 item 1.
305. *Id.*, Art. 69 para. 1 item 1.
306. *Id.*, Art. 69 para. 1 item 3.
307. *Id.*, Art. 31 para. 1.

352. Behavioural measures have aimed at eliminating an established infringement of competition or preventing its repetition. The Agency may impose following behavioural measures: measures for removing the established infringement of competition or for preventing occurrence thereof or similar infringement and undertaking particular action or prohibition to undertake a particular action.[308] Any such measure must be proportionate to the gravity of the infringement committed and directly related to the acts or practices that caused the infringement.[309]

353. Structural measures may be imposed when the Agency established the existence of impairment of competition and a substantial risk of repeating the same or similar infringement as a direct consequence of the structure of the undertaking.[310] The Agency may order a measure aimed at changing the structure of the undertaking with a view to removing such risk or restoring the structure which existed before the occurrence of established infringement.

354. Structural measures shall only be imposed under the following conditions:

(1) if it is not possible to impose equally or similarly effective behavioural remedy or if imposing behavioural remedy would be more burdensome for the undertaking than the specific structural remedy, or
(2) if a previously imposed behavioural remedy in respect of the same infringement was not fully implemented.[311]

355. The structural measures may be measures of selling (transfer or disposal) the existing company, a part thereof or a group of companies to other persons who are not connected to the undertaking whom these measures concern; terminating the agreement on joint venture and establishment of a company; terminating personal connection (management bodies and decision-making bodies in a company) as well as other measures in accordance with the law.[312]

VI. Interim Measures

356. The Competition Act gives the possibility to the Agency to impose a measure aimed at eliminating an infringement of competition before it reaches a final decision on the merits. Interim measures can be ordered if the practices or acts which are subject to the proceedings pose a risk of irreparable damage to persons whom such practices and acts directly concern. The Agency may order interim measures to cease such practices or enforce such acts and/or obligations to take actions or refrain from actions preventing or eliminating their harmful effects.[313]

---

308. *Id.*, Art. 59 para. 1.
309. *Id.*, Art. 59 para. 2.
310. *Id.*, Art. 59 para. 3.
311. *Id.*, Art. 59 para. 4.
312. *Id.*, Art. 59 para. 5.
313. *Id.*, Art. 44 para. 1.

357. The Director of the Agency, by the conclusion, is authorized to adopt the interim measures.[314] Interim measures may last until the adoption of the decision of the Agency.[315]

358. However, at least two important questions are not answered by the Competition Act in regulating this institute. First, there is no regulation which gives answer what is going to happen if undertakings breached the decision ordering interim measures. Also, there is no answer whether undertakings have the right to appeal on the decision on interim measure. Based on the interpretation of the other provisions of the Competition Act, in this case, the interested party may bring an administrative dispute.

VII. Commitments Procedure

359. The Agency has the possibility to suspend proceedings based on the commitments offered by the investigated party. During the proceedings and no later than thirty days from the day of delivering notice of established facts, circumstances and conclusions in the proceedings, the party to the proceedings may propose to the Agency measures, conditions and time limits to remove adverse effects of its acts or omissions to act.[316]

360. Agency is not obliged to accept the party's proposal of the commitments. The Competition Act prescribes that the Agency shall accept the party's proposal of the commitments provided that the following conditions are cumulatively fulfilled:

(1) the impairment of competition lasted for a short time;[317]
(2) the party to the proceedings fully cooperates with the Agency;[318]
(3) the proceedings include a large number of parties,[319] and
(4) the cost-effectiveness of the proceedings is ensured.[320]

361. If the Agency accepts party's proposal of the commitments, it will be by decision, order implementation of the proposed measures, as well as the conditions and time limits for their implementation.[321] By the same decision, the Agency shall also set a time limit by which the party is obliged to submit evidence that the ordered measures and conditions were complied with within time limits set in the

314. *Id.*, Art. 44 para. 2.
315. *Id.*, Art. 44 para. 3.
316. *Id.*, Art. 45 para. 1.
317. *Id.*, Art. 45 para. 4 item 1.
318. *Id.*, Art. 45 para. 4 item 2.
319. *Id.*, Art. 45 para. 4 item 3.
320. *Id.*, Art. 45 para. 4 item 4.
321. *Id.*, Art. 45 para. 2.

decision.[322] In any case, the Agency may not accept the proposal if the party to the proceedings generated considerable profit by the infringement of competition in question.[323]

362. The Agency ex officio monitors whether the party is complying with the commitments. The Agency shall be obliged to re-open the proceedings if: (1) there has been a material change in any of the circumstances on which the Agency decision was based and/or if the decision was based on incorrect or false information; (2) the party does not comply with the commitments.[324] Further, in the text will be presented the instances of the Agency's application of this principle.[325]

§2. Civil Enforcement

I. Competent Civil Courts

363. There are no specialized courts for competition law disputes in Montenegro.

364. In accordance with Law on Courts, the Commercial Court is competent in competition law issues. Law on Courts has explicit norm which states that the Commercial Court shall hear and determine at first instance disputes relating to distortion of competition, abuse of monopolistic or dominant position on the market and entering into monopolistic agreements.[326] Additionally, Commercial Court has jurisdiction in all disputes between companies, entrepreneurs and other legal persons performing economic activity (commercial entities), which arise from their commercial-legal relationships and in the disputes arising between commercial entities and other legal persons in the performance of the activity of commercial entities.[327] The Commercial Court is established for the territory of Montenegro, and its seat is in Podgorica.

365. Basic courts do not have competence in competition law issues in Montenegro. This is evident from comparing jurisdiction of the Commercial Court with the norm which said that basic courts should have jurisdiction to decide at first instance in other matters as well unless the jurisdiction of another court is prescribed by law.[328]

322. *Id.*, Art. 45 para. 2.
323. *Id.*, Art. 45 para. 5.
324. *Id.*, Art. 45 para. 6.
325. *See* Part II, Ch. 1, §1, A below.
326. Law on Courts, Art. 18 para. 1 item 7.
327. *Id.*, Art. 18 para. 1 item 7.
328. *Id.*, Art. 14 para. 2.

366. Appellate Court decides on appeals against decisions of commercial courts.[329] The Appellate Court is established for the territory of Montenegro, and its seat is in Podgorica.

367. Second instance decisions of the Appellate Court are final. The decisions of these courts may, in certain cases, be challenged before the Supreme Court by way of an extraordinary remedy of revision (in Montenegrin: *revizija*). In accordance with Law on Civil Procedure, parties may file a request for revision of the final and enforceable judgment of the court of second instance within thirty days from the day of the delivery of the judgment.[330]

368. The general rule is that the revision is not allowed in property disputes where the statement of claims relates to an amount of money, delivery of an object or committing some other action if the value of the disputed matter in the contested part of the final and enforceable judgment does not exceed the amount of EUR 20,000.[331] However, the revision shall always be allowed, *inter alia*, in property disputes arising from unconstitutional and illegal individual acts and actions by which legal or natural persons are placed in an unfair position in the market due to their seat or place of permanent residence or the market is violated in some other manner, involving disputes on the compensation of damage caused by it.[332]

369. The general rule is that revision can be lodged only for certain substantial violation of provisions of the civil procedure or misapplication of substantive law. Revision may be not requested for erroneously or incompletely determined facts.[333] In any event, revision does not suspend enforcement of a final judgment.[334]

II. Sanctions

A. *Nullity*

370. General rules regarding the nullity of a contract are provided in Law on Obligations.[335] It states that a contract contrary to mandatory legislation or morals of the society shall be null and void unless the purpose of the rule violated refers to another sanction, or unless the law provides for something else in the specific case.[336]

---

329. Law on Courts, Art. 20 para. 1 item 1.
330. Law on Civil Procedure (*Zakon o parničnom postupku, Službeni list Crne Gore* 022/04, 028/05, 076/06, 073/10, 047/15, 051/17, 062/18, 034/19 and 042/19), Art. 397 para. 1.
331. *Id.*, Art. 397 para. 2.
332. *Id.*, Art. 397 para. 4 item 3.
333. *Id.*, Art. 400 para. 2.
334. *Id.*, Art. 399.
335. Law on Obligations (*Zakon o obligacionim odnosima, Službeni list Crne Gore* 047/08, 004/11 and 022/17).
336. *Id.*, Art. 101 para. 1.

371. In the case of nullity of the contract, each contracting party shall restitute to the other that what is received on the ground of such a contract. Should this be not feasible, or should the nature of that what has been performed prevent restituting, adequate compensation in money shall be given according to prices at the time of passing the court decision unless otherwise provided by law. In deciding, the court shall consider the good faith of each and both parties, the significance of endangered good or interests, as well as the existing conceptions of morality.[337]

372. Nullity of a contractual provision shall not imply nullity of the contract itself if it can stand without the null provision and should such provision be neither a condition for contract nor a decisive reason for making it. Moreover, the contract shall remain effective even should the null provision be a requirement or a decisive motive of contract, in case if the nullity was established exactly in order for the contract to be exempted from such provision and to become valid without it.[338]

373. A null and void contract shall not become valid if the prohibition or other cause of nullity subsequently disappeared. However, nullity shall not be claimed should the prohibition be of minor importance and after the contract has been performed.[339]

374. Law on Obligations states that the court ex officio take account of potential nullity and nullity may be claimed by every person interested, including the public prosecutor.[340] The right to claim nullity does not become extinguished.[341]

375. A similar provision can be found in Competition Act which proclaims that restrictive agreements are prohibited and null and void, except in cases determined by the Law (block exemption or by to a decision granting an individual exemption).[342] The operative part of an Agency decision establishing the existence of a restrictive agreement always contains a holding that the agreement is null and void.

B. Damages

376. Institute of the antitrust damages actions is not sufficiently developed in Montenegro. The main reason should be found in insufficient regulation of antitrust damages.

337. *Id.*, Art. 102 para. 3.
338. *Id.*, Art. 103.
339. *Id.*, Art. 105.
340. *Id.*, Art. 107.
341. *Id.*, Art. 108.
342. Competition Act, Art. 8.

377. In accordance with Montenegrin law, a claim for antitrust damages has to be an action in tort (delict), based on the general provisions of the Law on Obligations. One of the main principles of the Law on Obligations is that everyone is obliged to refrain from any acts which may cause damage to another.[343]

378. In order to have success in a tort action, a plaintiff has to prove the following: (1) the existence of a tortuous act, (2) damage suffered, (3) existence of fault and (4) the causal link between the act and the damage.[344] Fault exists if a person caused injury or loss intentionally or out of negligence.

379. In assessing whether a person causing injury or loss is at fault, the court shall take account of the regular course of events, and how reasonable and careful man would be expected to act in given circumstances.[345] The fault of the tortfeasor is presumed, but he may rebut the presumption. Law explicitly prescribes that whoever causes injury or loss to another shall be liable to compensate it unless he proves that the damage was caused without his fault.[346]

380. The Competition Act contains a general provision in relation to compensation of damages. The Competition Act prescribes that the compensation for damage caused by the acts and practices constituting impairment of competition which is established by decision of the Agency shall be exercised in a civil suit before the competent court.[347]

381. From this article, but also taking in account overall legal system in Montenegro, it is evident that the Agency is not competent to decide on damages, and this right is in the hands of the competent court. However, it is unclear whether the decision of the Agency assumes that the damage has occurred, or it has to be proven in court proceedings.

382. For the Agency, the existence of a restrictive agreement is a prerequisite for initiating misdemeanour proceedings and imposing appropriate administrative sanctions. In the event that a proceeding for compensation for damages under a restrictive agreement is initiated before the competent court, based on the stated norms from the Law on Obligations, it is the duty of the court to take care of the nullity of the contract ex officio.

383. According to Law on Civil Procedure, when the court's decision depends on preliminary ruling on the matter as to the existence of a certain right or legal relationship and such a decision has not yet been rendered by the court or another competent authority (preliminary matter) the court itself may resolve the matter unless

343. Law on Obligations, Art. 8.
344. Snežana Miladinović, *Pravo za ekonomiste* [*Law for Economists*] 160–165 (2012).
345. Law on Obligations, Art. 152.
346. *Id.*, Art. 148 para. 1.
347. *Id.*, Art. 65.

otherwise stipulated by special regulations. Court decision on a preliminary matter shall have legal effect only in the litigation in which that matter has been determined.[348]

384. Therefore, in this case, provided that the proceedings for establishing impairment of competition are initiated before the Agency, the court should suspend the proceedings and wait for the Agency to resolve the nullity of the agreement.

C. Interim Measures

385. The Competition Act regulates the issue of interim measures which the Agency may impose during the administrative proceedings which conduct. However, interim measures can be imposed by a civil court, in the process of private enforcement of the competition legislation.

386. In relation to this matter in Montenegro, it can be distinguished two types of interim measures which can be imposed by Court: (1) measures aimed at securing the claim and (2) measures aimed at preservation of evidence.

387. Measures aimed at securing the claim are regulated by Law on Enforcement and Security.[349] According to this Law, the public enforcement officer is competent to decide in enforcement procedure, to levy enforcement, as well as to enforce securing of claims, except in the cases that competency of the court is prescribed for by law.[350] However, the Court may upon the creditor's petition, and in the presence of certain conditions, issue interim measures for securing a monetary claim. The court may order an interim measure prior to initiation and during the court or administrative procedure, as well as upon termination of such procedures until the enforcement is levied.[351]

388. Interim measure for securing a monetary claim may be ordered if: (i) the creditor made the existence of claim probable and (ii) there is the danger that without such a measure the debtor shall prevent or significantly hamper the collection of a claim, by divesting of, concealing, or disposing of his property or assets.[352] The second requirement does not apply if the creditor makes probable that by the proposed measure, the debtor would suffer only insignificant damage.[353] Upon creditor's motion, the court may order an interim measure even in the absence of these two conditions, if he previously deposits, within the specified deadline, the amount determined by the court as surety for damage that could be incurred to the debtor

348. Law on Civil Procedure, Art. 14.
349. Law on Enforcement and Security (*Zakon o izvršenju i obezbjeđenju, Službeni list Crne Gore* 036/11, 028/14, 020/15, 022/17, 076/17 and 025/19).
350. *Id.*, Art. 3 para. 1.
351. *Id.*, Art. 278.
352. *Id.*, Art. 287 para. 1.
353. *Id.*, Art. 287 para. 2.

by ordering and implementing the interim relief.[354] However, the debtor is entitled to compensation by a creditor for the damage incurred to him by an interim measure for which it has been determined that it is groundless or that has not been justified by the creditor.[355]

389. Law on Enforcement and Security explicitly states that the court may order any measure capable of securing the collection of the monetary claim and then provides *exempli causa* with the following list of interim measures: (1) prohibition imposed on the debtor to dispose of movable assets, as well as the safekeeping of such assets;[356] (2) prohibition to dispose of and encumber shares or holdings in a business organization, with the registration of prohibition in the relevant registry;[357] (3) prohibition imposed on the debtor to divest of or encumber his immovable property or property rights registered on the immovable property in the immovable property cadastre for his benefit, with the registration of prohibition in the immovable property cadastre;[358] (4) restraint the debtor's debtor from making payments to the debtor;[359] (5) order to a bank not to make payments from the debtor's account to the debtor or third person.[360]

390. Interim measures can also be issued in support of a non-monetary claim. For the purpose of securing a non-monetary claim, an interim measure may be ordered, if: (i) creditor made probable the existence of claim and (ii) danger that the satisfaction of claim shall be otherwise prevented or be significantly hampered.[361] Interim measures may also be ordered when a creditor makes probable that the measure is needed in order to prevent the use of force or occurrence of irreparable damage. The same conditions for imposing interim measure for securing a monetary claim apply to interim measure for securing a non-monetary claim.

391. Measures for the preservation of evidence are regulated by the Law on Civil Procedure. In case of the justified belief that a piece of evidence will not be available for presentation or that its later presentation may be hindered, it may be proposed that such evidence be presented in the course of and prior to instituting the litigation. In the pleading on request for the provision of evidence, the applicant shall indicate facts to be proved, evidence to be presented and reasons for believing that the later presentation of evidence will not be possible or that the presentation shall be hindered.[362] It is not allowed to appeal against the court ruling on acceptance of the motion for the provision of evidence.[363]

354. *Id.*, Art. 282 para. 1.
355. *Id.*, Art. 286.
356. *Id.*, Art. 288 para. 1 item 1.
357. *Id.*, Art. 288 para. 1 item 2.
358. *Id.*, Art. 288 para. 1 item 3.
359. *Id.*, Art. 288 para. 1 item 4.
360. *Id.*, Art. 288 para. 1 item 5.
361. *Id.*, Art. 289 para. 1.
362. Law on Civil Procedure, Art. 268.
363. *Id.*, Art. 269 para. 6.

§3. CRIMINAL ENFORCEMENT

I. Criminal Sanctions for Antitrust Violations

A. Criminal Liability of Individuals

392. Montenegrin Criminal Code which is in force from 2003, contains special criminal act 'Abuse of monopoly position'. This criminal act is Part 23 of the Criminal Code titled 'Criminal offences against payment transactions and business operations' (in Montenegrin: *Krivična djela protiv platnog prometa i privrednog poslovanja*).[364]

393. Criminal code criminalizes the abuse of monopoly or dominant market position or concluding monopolistic contracts. The subject of this criminal act is a responsible officer in a business entity or other business enterprise.

394. The wrongdoers of this criminal act would most plausibly be directors or other responsible persons in accordance with the internal act of business entities. Their intent to commit this offence has to be proven. At least two conditions have to be met in order to establish the existence of this criminal offence: (1) a responsible officer in a business entity or other business enterprise has to abuse monopoly or dominant market position or cause market disruptions or put that entity into a favoured position in relation to others by concluding monopolistic contracts; and (2) has to obtain pecuniary gain for that entity or for another, or cause damage to other business enterprises. It is not a punishable attempt to unlawfully restrict competition.[365]

395. The crime is punishable by six months to five years' imprisonment. A fine is not prescribed for this criminal offence in Montenegro.[366]

396. The general principle is that courts fix the punishment for the perpetrator of a criminal offence within the statutory limits for that particular offence, taking into account the purpose of punishment. Furthermore, in fixing the punishment, the court considers all circumstances which have an influence on the grading of the sentence (mitigating and aggravating circumstances), and in particular: the degree of culpability, motives for the commission of the offence, degree of peril or injury to the protected good, circumstances under which the offence was committed, perpetrator's history, his personal situation, his behaviour after the commission of the criminal offence, particularly his attitude towards the victim of the criminal offence as well as any other circumstances concerning the perpetrator's personality.[367] The court may impose on a perpetrator a punishment below the limit laid down by law

364. Montenegrin Criminal Code (*Krivični zakonik Crne Gore, Službeni list Crne Gore* 070/03, 013/04, 047/06, 040/08, 032/11, 040/13, 014/15, 044/17 and 049/18).
365. *Id.*, Art. 270.
366. *Id.*, Art. 270.
367. *Id.*, Art. 42.

or a lighter punishment provided that: (1) a lighter punishment is provided for by law;[368] (2) remission of punishment is provided for by law, but the punishment does not get remitted by the court;[369] (3) it is established that there were particularly mitigating circumstances, and it is assessed that a mitigated punishment will be sufficient to achieve the purpose of punishment.[370] Finally, the court may release from the sentence a perpetrator where a perpetrator committed a criminal offence punishable by maximum five-year prison term provided that after the commission of criminal offence but before he learned he was uncovered he had eliminated the consequences of the offence or had compensated the damage inflicted by the criminal offence.[371]

397. Criminal prosecution of this criminal act may take place within five years after the offence had been committed.[372]

398. In the near future, it should be initiated to make the link between criminal responsibility under the Criminal act and leniency programme under the Competition Act. This connection needs to regulate situation which exculpates the perpetrator who satisfies the conditions for immunity within the meaning of the Competition Act from criminal responsibility.

B. Criminal Liability of Legal Persons

399. Criminal Code regulates criminal responsibility for individual persons who engaged in criminal offence abuse of monopoly position. However, the undertaking engaging in the abuse of monopoly position within the meaning of the Criminal Code act may also be liable for a criminal act, under the Law on Criminal Liability of Legal Entities.[373] The Montenegro state authorities and local government authorities may not be liable for a criminal offence. Also, legal entity vested with public powers shall not be liable for a criminal offence committed in the performance of such powers.[374]

400. According to Law on Criminal Liability of Legal Entities, a legal entity shall be liable for a criminal offence of a responsible person who acted within his/her authorities on behalf of the legal entity with the intention to obtain any gain for the legal entity.[375] The legal entity shall be held liable for a criminal offence even

368. *Id.*, Art. 45 para. 1 item 1.
369. *Id.*, Art. 45 para. 1 item 2.
370. *Id.*, Art. 45 para. 1 item 3.
371. *Id.*, Art. 47 para. 3.
372. *Id.*, Art. 124 para. 1 item 5.
373. Law on Criminal Liability of Legal Entities (*Zakon o odgovornosti pravnih lica za krivicna djela, Službeni list Crne Gore* 002/07, 013/07, 073/10, 030/12 and 039/16).
374. *Id.*, Art. 2.
375. *Id.*, Art. 5.

if the responsible person who committed such criminal offence has not been convicted of such criminal offence.[376] Liability of a legal entity shall not exclude criminal liability of a responsible person for the criminal offence committed.[377]

401. A legal entity under bankruptcy may be liable for a criminal offence regardless of whether such an offence has been committed before or during the bankruptcy proceeding. In such a case, no punishment shall be pronounced, but the seizure of material gain or a security measure of seizure of items shall be imposed.[378]

402. A legal entity may be imposed the following sanctions for the criminal offence: (1) punishment; (2) suspended sentences; (3) security measures.[379] A legal entity may be imposed the following punishments: (i) fine and (ii) dissolution of the legal entity.[380] Fine and dissolution of a legal entity may be imposed only as principal punishments.[381] A fine shall be determined depending on the amount of the damage caused or illicit material gain obtained, and if these amounts are different, the higher amount shall serve as a basis for the determination of fine.[382] Fine may not be less than the two-fold amount of the damage caused or illicit material gain obtained or higher than the 100-fold amount of the material damage caused or illicit material gain obtained.[383] The penalty of dissolution of a legal entity may be ordered if the business conducted by the legal entity was wholly or considerably in the function of committing the criminal offence. The liquidation proceeding shall be conducted in companies along with the imposing of the penalty of dissolution of a legal entity.[384]

403. For criminal offences for which legal entities are held liable, the following security measures may be imposed: (1) developing and implementing the programme of effective, necessary and reasonable measures; (2) seizure of items; (3) publication of the sentence; (4) ban on conducting certain business or other activities.[385] In addition, the following legal consequences of a conviction may come into effect for a legal person: (1) ban on conducting an activity on the basis of a permit, licence, authorization or concession issued by state authorities; (2) ban on getting a permit, licence, authorization or concession issued by state authorities.[386]

404. This legal act recognizes three situations for exemption from punishment: (1) if the legal entity reveals and reports a criminal offence before finding out that

---

376. *Id.*, Art. 6 para. 1.
377. *Id.*, Art. 6 para. 2.
378. *Id.*, Art. 7.
379. *Id.*, Art. 12.
380. *Id.*, Art. 13 para. 1.
381. *Id.*, Art. 13 para. 2.
382. *Id.*, Art. 14 para. 1.
383. *Id.*, Art. 14 para. 2.
384. *Id.*, Art. 22.
385. *Id.*, Art. 28 para. 1.
386. *Id.*, Art. 33 para. 1.

the criminal proceedings were initiated; (2) if upon the committing of the criminal offence the legal entity voluntarily and immediately returns the illegally obtained material gain or rectifies the harmful consequences caused or delivers data significant for liability of another legal entity with which it is not connected organizationally; (3) if the legal entity has undertaken all the effective, necessary and reasonable measures aimed at preventing and revealing the commission of the criminal offence.[387]

405. Generally, this type of criminal responsibility is not recognized in the practice of Montenegrin courts. No legal person has ever been found to be criminally responsible for an antitrust infringement.

II. Other Application of Criminal Law to Relevant Conduct

406. In the separate article described above Criminal Code regulates the special offence 'Abuse of monopoly position' and prescribes sanctions for its commission. In the event of the commission of a criminal offence of abuse of monopoly position, many other general provisions of Criminal Code in Montenegro may apply. However, in relation to this offence, there are no other specific provisions that directly regulate criminal liability in cases of violation of competition law.

III. Role of Prosecutors

407. Criminal proceedings are initiated and conducted in line with the indictment of an authorized prosecutor. The basic right and the main duty of the State prosecutor is the prosecution of criminal offenders. The role of prosecutors is regulated by the Criminal procedure code.[388] For criminal offences that are prosecuted ex officio, the authorized prosecutor is the State prosecutor whereas, for criminal offences prosecuted upon a private action, the authorized prosecutor is a private prosecutor.[389] If a State prosecutor determines that there are no grounds for the institution or conduct of criminal proceedings, the injured party acting as a subsidiary prosecutor may assume his/her role.[390] The State prosecutor shall initiate prosecution when there is reasonable suspicion that a certain person has committed a criminal offence that is prosecuted ex officio.[391]

408. The State prosecutor has wide powers in criminal proceedings. They are authorized, *inter alia*, to: (i) issue binding orders or directly manage the activities of the administrative authority competent for police affairs, tax and customs authorities in the preliminary investigation; (ii) order the investigation to be conducted,

---

387. *Id.*, Art. 23.
388. Criminal Procedure Code (*Zakonik o krivičnom postupku, Službeni list Crne Gore* 057/09, 049/10, 047/14, 002/15 and 028/18).
389. *Id.*, Art. 18 para. 2.
390. *Id.*, Art. 18 para. 3.
391. *Id.*, Art. 19.

conduct the investigation and perform urgent evidentiary actions during the preliminary investigation; (iii) conclude agreements on the admission of guilt with accused persons; (iv) present and represent indictments before competent courts; (v) lodge legal remedies against judgments.[392]

409. State prosecutors have unfortunately been inactive in prosecuting offences against competition which could be largely attributed to the lack of initiative and knowledge in competition law cases. Also, the lack of clear definition of the criminal offence of the abuse of monopoly position in Article 270 of the Criminal Code can be stated as one of the arguments for the lack of more efficient criminal prosecution in these cases.

IV. Competent Criminal Courts

410. The competence of courts in criminal matters depends on the threatened sanction. In accordance to Law on Courts, in criminal cases, basic courts have jurisdiction to hear and determine at first instance criminal offences punishable by law by a fine or imprisonment of up to ten years as principal punishment, regardless of the character, profession and position of the person against whom the proceedings are conducted.[393] The basic court has jurisdiction to hear in first instance cases involving criminal act 'Abuse of monopoly position' from Article 270 of the Criminal Code.

411. For criminal offences for which the prescribed principal punishment is a fine or imprisonment for a term of up to ten years, a single judge shall adjudicate in the first instance, with the exception of offences of the organized crime.[394] The second instance courts shall adjudicate in a panel composed of three judges. The third instance courts shall adjudicate in a panel composed of five judges.[395]

412. The general rule regarding territorial jurisdiction in Montenegrin criminal proceedings law is that competent court is the court on whose territory the criminal act was committed or attempted.[396] A private action may be filed with the court within the territory of which the accused person has a permanent or a temporary residence.[397] If the criminal offence was committed or attempted within the territory of several courts or on the border of those territories, or if it is uncertain within which territory the offence has been committed or attempted, the court which on the indictment of the authorized prosecutor has first instituted the procedure shall have jurisdiction.[398]

392. *Id.*, Art. 44.
393. Law on Courts, Art. 14 para. 1 item 1.
394. Criminal Procedure Code, Art. 24 para. 2.
395. *Id.*, Art. 24 para. 4.
396. *Id.*, Art. 25 para. 1.
397. *Id.*, Art. 25 para. 2.
398. *Id.*, Art. 25 para. 3.

413. If the place of the commission of a criminal offence is unknown or if this place is not in the territory of Montenegro, the competent court shall be the one within whose territory the accused person has temporary or permanent residence.[399] That court retains jurisdiction even after the place of the commission of the criminal offence has become known. If neither the place of the commission of the criminal offence nor the temporary or permanent residence of the accused person is known, or if both of them are outside the territory of Montenegro, the competent court shall be the one within whose territory the accused person is deprived of liberty or turned himself/herself in.[400] If a person has committed a criminal offence both in Montenegro and abroad, the competent court shall be the one that has jurisdiction over the criminal offence committed in Montenegro.[401] If it is impossible to determine which court has territorial jurisdiction in a specific case, the Supreme Court designates one of the courts of real jurisdiction as the court competent to conduct the proceedings.[402] There are additional rules on territorial jurisdiction – territorial jurisdiction of courts in cases of offences committed on a national vessel or aircraft;[403] and territorial jurisdiction of courts in cases committed by means of media.[404]

399. *Id.*, Art. 28 para. 1.
400. *Id.*, Art. 28 para. 3.
401. *Id.*, Art. 29.
402. *Id.*, Art. 30.
403. *Id.*, Art. 26.
404. *Id.*, Art. 27.

Part II. Application of the Prohibition

414. Based on Article 61 of the Competition Act, the Agency is required to publish operating parts of its decisions on its website. Therefore, in Montenegro, the full texts of the Agency's decisions are not publicly available, so it is impossible to determine the Agency's legal reasoning in determining violations of competition law. In addition, the Agency's annual activity reports for the period 2013–2018 served as a source of analysis in this part of the monograph where individual cases are dealt with in more detail. In this part of the monograph will be described the cases of impairment of competition and the legal actions taken by the Agency that were available during the writing of the monograph.

415. The implementation is the most important challenge in the application of competition law in Montenegro. For the time being, Montenegro lacks more effective enforcement of the law in all areas of competition law. The aforementioned fact of the lack of proper practice further influenced the quality and scope of this part of the monograph. The following are all publicly available cases of violation of competition law in the period 2012–2018.

Chapter 1. Restrictive Agreements

416. When it comes to cartel agreements establishing impairment of competition, they have been available on the Agency's website and in the Annual Activity Reports, since 2012, when the Competition Act came into force.

417. To our knowledge, there were no cases of impairment of competition in restrictive agreements before 2012. In the period after 2012, the Agency investigated and determined the existence of cartel agreements in a number of cases. However, as it has been pointed out earlier, for the time being in Montenegro, we cannot speak of the Agency's established practice in investigating cartel agreements.

§1. Horizontal Agreements

I. Cartels

A. Price Fixing

1. Daily Newspapers

418. One of the first cases initiated by the Agency in the area of restrictive agreements after the adoption of the Competition Act concerns *price fixing* on the market of daily newspapers available to readers throughout Montenegro. With the conclusion of this cartel agreement, it was agreed to increase the prices of daily newspapers in the fixed amount from EUR/cents 50 to EUR/cents 70. The proceedings were initiated against the publishing company Daily Press Podgorica, Jumedia Mont Podgorica, Pobjeda Podgorica, Novosti Pres Podgorica, Media Nea Podgorica, Ringier Axel Springer Belgrade (Stari Grad).

419. The Agency has determined the conclusion of the prohibited cartel agreement by the four largest undertakings of printed dailies available in the entire territory of Montenegro (Daily Press-News, Jumedia Mont-Dan, Media Nea-Dnevne novine and Pobjeda).[405] The Agency has instructed the aforementioned business entities to determine the price of their daily printed newspapers independently within thirty days from the date of delivery of the decision. The proceedings against two parties to the cartel agreement, which were the subject of the Agency's action, were suspended due to lack of material evidence on participation in the prohibited agreement.

420. In this case, the inefficiency of the Montenegrin legal system in sanctioning cases of impairment of competition was highlighted. It is important to point out the sequence of actions taken by the Agency and interested parties in this case.

405. Agency Decision No. 02 – UPI-24/168-13 of 25 Apr. 2013, available at (in Montenegrin): http://www.azzk.me/1/doc/Rjesenje%20dnevne%20novine%20zast.podaci%20izreka.pdf (last accessed 11 Oct. 2019).

Namely, after establishing the existence of a prohibited agreement, the Agency filed a misdemeanour application with a request for the imposition of a misdemeanour sentence by the competent regional body for misdemeanours. The company Pobjeda Podgorica and the responsible person in this company were fined for the offence.

421. The regional misdemeanour body suspended the three proceedings initiated by the Decision on the statute of limitations for conducting the misdemeanour proceedings (against legal entities of Daily Press-Vijesti, Jumedia Mont-Dan and Media Nea-Dnevne novine and responsible persons in those legal entities). The Agency appealed to the Misdemeanour Council against decisions in two cases filed against legal entities Daily Press-Vijesti and Jumedia Mont-Dan, while it withdrew from the proceedings against Media Nea-Dnevna Novine for the lack of a substance of misdemeanour under the old Law on Protection of Competition. The Misdemeanour Council rejected the Agency's complaints. Following this, the Agency filed a motion with the Supreme State Prosecutor's Office to file a petition for protection of legality before the Supreme Court of Montenegro against the Decision of the Misdemeanour Council.[406] The Supreme Court of Montenegro's ruling rejected as unfounded a petition for protection of legality of the Supreme State Prosecutor's Office.

2. Driving Schools

422. The last publicly available decision in relation to *price-fixing*, which established a cartel agreement by the Agency, concerns driving schools from the territory of the municipality of Nikšić.[407] In this ex officio proceedings, the subject of the Agency's research was the Decision on a new price list of the driver training for all vehicle categories as of 13 April 2017. The Agency found that the said decision had elements of a cartel agreement and declared it prohibited and null and void. This decision was made jointly by the following driving schools: Zeleni signal, Klikas, Tadić, Zarubica Company, Gold, Filip, and Lucky Driver. All of these driving schools are active in the market of providing driver training services for all categories of vehicles in the territory of the municipality of Niksic. With the same Decision, the Agency instructed the aforementioned driving schools to make decisions on the price of services and conditions independently and irrespective of their competitors, in a clear and transparent manner, and that for a period of two years, notify the Agency on any change in the decision or the adoption of a new price list decision within seven days from the date of application.

406. Agency's Annual Report for 2014, p. 38.
407. Agency Decision No. 02-UPI-8/65-18 of 15 Oct. 2018, available at (in Montenegrin): http://www.azzk.me/1/doc/rjesenja%20zabranjeni%20sporazumi/2018-10-15_Rjesenje%20auto%20skole.pdf (last accessed 11 Oct. 2019).

3. Šafran Case

423. In the case of Šafran, the subject of the Agency's analysis was the Agreement on the use of the Šafran trademark and the protection of the buyer for resale. The agreement was concluded between the companies Šafran Bar and Obuća Minja. As in previous cases, the rationale of the Agency's decision was not publicly available, so the analysis was made on the basis of the publicly available annual report of the Agency for 2014, which in this case did not contain complete information on the said case.

424. In 2014, the Agency determined that certain provisions of this Agreement were intended to prevent, restrict or distort competition in the relevant market.[408] Specifically, under the provisions of the concluded Agreement, Šafran Bar had the right to supervise and coordinate the application of the sales price of its buyers to end-users for products of Šafran brand. In accordance with Article 8 of the Law on Protection of Competition, the Agency declared certain parts of the Agreement prohibited and null and void. In this case, the Agency prohibited further application and enforcement of the provisions of the Agreement. Also, the company Šafran Bar was forbidden to determine, coordinate and supervise the application of the sales price on the market of its buyers to end-users for products of Šafran brand. A petition to initiate misdemeanour proceedings against these companies was filed with the Regional Misdemeanour Bodies in Bar and Berane.

4. Price-Fixing in Bid-Rigging Context

425. Based on publicly announced decisions and insight into regular annual reports, it can be seen that the Agency has so far determined the existence of a cartel agreement in three cases in the public procurement procedure. In the first case, it was a cartel agreement in the insurance market. Namely, in 2015, the Agency issued a decision establishing the existence of a cartel agreement between two independent legal entities registered for performing insurance activities on the territory of Montenegro.[409] During the procedure, the Agency found that the insurance companies Sava Montenegro and Lovcen osiguranje entered into several cartel-type agreements, namely: an agreement on a joint appearance on the Montenegrin market (as an umbrella agreement), and then an individual ad hoc contract for public procurement of insurance of persons and property services of the Montenegrin Electric Transmission System (in Montenegrin: *Crnogorski elektroprenosni sistem*).

426. The agreements also provided for risk-bearing by submitting a joint offer of two direct competitors in the insurance market in Montenegro. In its Annual

408. Agency Decision No. 02-UPI-36/19-14 of 30 Dec. 2015, available at (in Montenegrin): http://www.azzk.me/1/doc/Rjesenje_safran-obuca%20minja.pdf (last accessed 11 Oct. 2019).

409. Agency Decision No. 02-UPI-20/39-15 of 24 Jul. 2015, available at (in Montenegrin): http://www.azzk.me/1/doc/rjesenja%20zabranjeni%20sporazumi/Rjesenje_osiguranje.pdf (last accessed 11 Oct. 2019).

Report for 2014, the Agency pointed out that this type of agreement on the joint appearance of large companies is detrimental to contracting entities, public companies with a direct effect of potential damage to the operation of public enterprises.[410] According to the Agency's rationale, Lovćen Osiguranje and Sava Montenegro osiguranje were obliged to make business decisions and operate on the market independently, as well as to independently determine their prices, conditions of cooperation with buyers and/or contracting entities in public procurement procedures, irrespective of their competitors. It is also important to emphasize that the Agency's decision became final in this proceedings. Against the Agency's decision, the parties filed the lawsuit with the Administrative Court of Montenegro, which was rejected.[411] After the decision became final, a petition to initiate misdemeanour proceedings against these companies was filed with the Misdemeanour Court.

427. In the statement of claim filed with the Administrative Court, Sava Montenegro and Lovćen osiguranje stated that in the decision establishing the existence of the cartel agreement, the Agency took the position that all agreements on joint operation on the market of entities performing the same activities on the same market are null and void, in terms of the provisions of Article 8 of the Law on Protection of Competition. Considering that all contracts of this kind are prohibited, the Agency does not deal with the substance of the monopoly contracts in its decision, that is, it does not determine whether the contracts in question directly or indirectly determine purchase or sale prices or other terms of trade, whether the contracts restrict or control production, market, technical development or investment, nor whether the market or sources of supply are divided. In their view, the Agency's decision does not disclose the facts and actions that declare the contracts in question null and void, nor does it state the action which violated a specific norm in the Competition Act. They emphasized to the plaintiff that the contracts in question were concluded on the basis of Article 3 of the Law on Insurance and in accordance with Articles 79 and 80 of the Law on Public Procurement, which did not provide for any restrictions regarding the submission of a joint bid.[412] Their legal arguments stating that those were not prohibited agreements confirmed the letter of the ISA No. 04-318/3-15 from 29 July 2015 in which it was considered that, in the case at hand, these were not prohibited contracts. The main objective and motive of the joint bid, and in this respect of the joint contracts, was the joint coverage and risk distribution, taking into account the magnitude of the risk taken, and not in any way impairment of competition. In this proceeding, two-sector regulators had opposite views, which affected the quality of their cooperation in practice.[413]

428. In the rationale of the judgment of the Administrative Court, it was noted that the Agency determined that the conclusion of the agreement was to eliminate mutual competition and directly determine the common price of the two largest

410. Agency's Annual Report for 2014, pp. 42–44.
411. Administrative Court Judgment No. U. 2259/2015, not available online.
412. Law on Public Procurement (*Zakon o javnim nabavkama, Službeni list Crne Gore* 042/11, 057/14, 028/15, 042/17).
413. *See* Part I, Ch. 2, §2, III above.

competitors (over 55% of the market share) with the ultimate aim of preventing, restricting and distorting competition in the relevant market.

429. In 2015, the Agency ex officio initiated and terminated proceedings against companies Urion and Montemedicom.[414] During the proceedings, the Agency determined that the Agreement on joint appearance in the public procurement procedure of the Health Insurance Fund of Montenegro by Public Call No. 02/15 which was concluded on 29 April 2015 between these companies had a cartel character. By the decision of the Agency, the Contract in question was declared null and void, and the contracting parties were prohibited from its further application. During the proceedings, the Agency determined that the conclusion of the disputed contract on joint appearance in the process of specific public procurement was preceded by an agreement on price (price-fixing), commercial conditions, mutual division of goods according to the specification in the tender documentation, as well as a mutual division in terms of place and health care institution to which certain goods will be delivered.[415] A petition to initiate misdemeanour proceedings was filed against these companies with the competent Misdemeanour Court.

430. The companies Urion and Montemedicon were also subject to investigation by the Agency in 2018, due to the conclusion of a cartel agreement in the public procurement procedure. In 2018, the Agency issued a decision declaring that the companies Urion and Montemedicon violated competition in the public procurement procedure.[416] In the conducted proceedings, the Agency has determined that these economic entities have concluded the Agreement on joint appearance in the public procurement procedure of the Health Insurance Fund of Montenegro.

431. The Agency clearly stated that the said Agreement was concluded with the aim of eliminating competition between independent undertakings Urion and Montemedicon and that it aimed to divide the market, determine price, limit and control the market. In the opinion of the Agency, the object or effect of the Agreement was to make the offered price in a particular public procurement, to be higher per individual product than it would be in the case of the individual offer of each of the parties to the prohibited agreement, as a result of the agreement reached. Although the statements of reasons for the Agency's decisions are not publicly available, it can be concluded that in addition to price-fixing in these cases, there are elements of the market allocation.

---

414. Agency Decision No. 02-UPI-11/99-16 of 24 Nov. 2016, available at (in Montenegrin): http://www.azzk.me/1/doc/rjesenja%20zabranjeni%20sporazumi/2016-11 24_Rjesenje%20zabranjeni%20sporazum%20Urion%20Montemedicom.pdf (last accessed 11 Oct. 2019).
415. Agency's Annual Report for 2015, pp. 50–51.
416. Agency Decision No. 02-UPI-11/129-16 of 23 Mar. 2018, available at (in Montenegrin): http://www.azzk.me/1/doc/rjesenja%20zabranjeni%20sporazumi/2018-03-23_Urion-Montemedicom.pdf (last accessed 11 Oct. 2019).

5. Price-Fixing Resolved by Commitments

432. One investigation related to the *price-fixing* scheme ended on the basis of the party commitments. The case concerns a cartel agreement between the telecommunications operator Telenor and the company Radio Difuzni Centar (hereinafter 'RDC'). RDC is a 100% state-owned company providing access to electronic communication networks and providing electronic communication services. In 2013, the Agency initiated proceedings against Telenor and RDC on suspicion of a cartel agreement. The agreement in question stipulated the long-term right of the telecommunication operator Telenor to use the RDC infrastructure free of charge in a discriminatory manner towards other mobile operators, which could have resulted in a significantly different cost and investment structure of the participants. Following the analysis, the Agency imposed an obligation on RDC and Telenor to terminate the provisions of the existing Agreement. This is how the proceedings in this case ended. In this case, the Agency has, for the first time, applied the principle of accepting the commitment to fulfil certain measures and conditions referred to in Article 45 of the Competition Act.

6. Pending Cases

433. According to publicly available information, one investigation for determination of the infringement of competition law in the case of restrictive agreements is ongoing before the Agency. The Agency initiated proceedings against a Pin Montenegro, company involved in the sale of electronic devices, by way of examining a flyer issued by this company, and it determined that the prices advertised for electronic devices are identical for all business entities listed on the flyer.[417] The Agency approached the company from the flyer and analysed the state of competition in the market for the sale of electronic devices in the territory of Montenegro and found that the concluded agreements typically indicate the active role of the supplier in determining the retail prices of its resellers.

B. Market/Client Allocation

434. In 2014, the Agency initiated and terminated proceedings against the company Kontejnerski terminal i generalni tereti Bar and Ocean Montenegro Bar. The restrictive agreement, in this case, was established in the market for the provision of overseas cargo ships in the Port of Bar aquatorium. The Agency found that the contractual relationship of these companies was aimed at preventing the development of competitors and creating barriers to entry for new undertakings into the relevant market in question. Namely, both parties to the agreement undertook the

417. Agency Decision No. 04-UPI-36/1-19 of 17 Apr. 2019, http://www.azzk.me/1/doc/zakljucci%20pokretanje%20postupka/2019-04-17_Rjesenje%20o%20pokretanju%20postupka%20PIN%20MNE.pdf (last accessed 11 Oct. 2019).

obligation of the cross-exclusive provision of services with the obligation of non-competition with the aim of closing and dividing the market. The parties to the agreement timely submitted the Annex to the contract, which declared the prohibited provisions of the Service Agreement concluded between the Kontejnerski terminal i generalni tereti Bar and Ocean Montenegro Bar null and void.[418] A petition to initiate misdemeanour proceedings against these companies and responsible persons in a legal entity was filed with the Regional Misdemeanour Body in Bar.

C. Production/Innovation Limitation

435. In the practice of the Agency so far, there have been no cases concerning restrictive agreements aimed at limitation of production/innovation.

D. Group Boycott

436. In the practice of the Agency so far, there have been no cases concerning this type of restrictive agreements.

E. Collusion on Other Objects

437. In the practice of the Agency so far, there have been no cases concerning this type of restrictive agreements.

II. Information Exchange Practices

438. The Agency has so far not investigated or finalized any proceedings concerning the unauthorized exchange of information.

III. Cooperation Agreements

A. Research and Development

439. The Agency has not yet investigated any agreement on joint research and development.

440. As mentioned above, the Government of Montenegro adopted a block exemption decree applicable to R&D agreements (R&D BED). However, there are no guidelines on the evaluation of such agreements.

418. Agency's Annual Report for 2014, pp. 40–41.

441. For the purpose of the R&D BED research and development includes the acquisition of specific knowledge and skills in the production process, analysis, studies, including experimental production, technical testing, installation and use of certain equipment and the acquisition of intellectual property rights on the results achieved.[419]

442. The block exemption from the prohibition applies to horizontal agreements under Article 8 of the Competition Act concluded between two or more independent undertakings which have the object of assigning or transferring intellectual property rights for the purpose of: (1) joint research and development; (2) the joint financing of research and development; or (3) joint use of research and development results when those provisions of the agreement are necessary for the implementation of the subject matter of the agreement.[420]

443. For the purpose of the R&D BED, a research and development agreement is an agreement between two or more parties that includes: (1) joint research and development of a contract product or technology contract process, or joint use of the results of joint research and development; (2) joint use of the results of the research and development of the contract product or technology contract process based on an agreement previously concluded between the same contracting parties; (3) joint research and development of the contract product or technology contract process, excluding joint use of the results of the joint research and development; (4) co-financing the research and development of the contract product or technology contract process and joint use of the results of the joint research and development; (5) joint use of the results of investments in the research and development of a contract product or technology contract process based on a previously concluded agreement between the same contracting parties; or (6) jointly financing the research and development of the contract product or technology contract process, excluding joint use of the results of the joint research and development.[421]

444. Block exemption from prohibition does not apply to research and development agreements that directly or indirectly establish restrictions that aim to: (1) prohibit a party to the agreement from concluding a research and development agreement with a third party in a field which is not directly related to the subject matter of the agreement and the contract product; (2) limit volume of production or sales; (3) determine the resale price of the contract product or license the technology contract process to a third party; (4) restrict the geographical area or specific customer group to which the parties to the agreement have the right to passively sell the contract product or to license the technology contract process; (5) prohibit refusal to supply customers from the geographical area of another party to a research and development agreement or a specific customer group assigned to the other contracting party by virtue of the specialization of use.[422]

---

419. R&D BED, Art. 2 para. 1.
420. *Id.*, Art. 4.
421. *Id.*, Art. 3 para. 1 item 7.
422. *Id.*, Art. 7 para. 1.

445. In order to apply for the block exemption from the prohibition to the horizontal R&D agreement, the following conditions must be cumulatively met: (1) that the agreement establishes the right of all parties to the agreement to be able to access, without restrictions, the results of joint research and development or joint financing of research and development; (2) the agreement establishes the right of each party to the agreement to free access to knowledge and skills, if such knowledge and skills are necessary for the use of the results of research and development; (3) that the joint use of R&D results is directly related to results that represent an intellectual property or specific knowledge and skills that are decisive and necessary in the process of manufacturing a contract product or applying technology contract processes; (4) the agreement specifying the specialization of production of one party to the agreement provides for an obligation to supply all parties to the agreement, except in the case of joint distribution or the exclusive right of the manufacturer to distribute the product.[423]

446. In addition, even though there is no direct provision in the R&D BED, R&D agreements must also meet the four conditions for block exemption under Article 9 of the Competition Act (efficiency gains, fair share for consumers, the indispensability of the restrictions, and no elimination of competition).

447. Provided that the conditions of the R&D BED are met, the block exemption applies to the R&D period if the parties to the agreement are not competitors, that is, to a period of up to seven years from the placing on the market of the contract product when the joint use is agreed. After the expiry of this period, the block exemption may apply if the market share of the parties to the agreement is less than 25% in the relevant market.[424]

B. Specialization

448. The block exemption from the prohibition of horizontal specialization agreements is regulated by the Specialization BED.

449. For the purpose of the Specialization BED, a specialization agreement may be: (1) a unilateral specialization agreement – where one contracting party agrees to fully or partly cease or refrain from the manufacturing of a particular product and to purchase those products from the other contracting party which undertakes to produce and supply those products; (2) a reciprocal specialization agreement where two or more parties undertake to cease or refrain from manufacturing different products and purchasing those products from each other whereby each party to the agreement undertakes to produce and supply those products; (3) a joint production agreement where two or more contracting parties agree on joint manufacturing.[425]

423. *Id.*, Art. 5 para. 1.
424. *Id.*, Art. 6.
425. Specialization BED, Art. 2 para. 1.

450. Block exemption applies to specialization agreements if the contracting parties: (1) accept the exclusive purchase or exclusive sale obligation or (2) jointly distribute the subject matter of the specialization.[426]

451. Agreements that qualify for the block exemption may be exempted from the prohibition if the parties' joint market share in the agreement does not exceed 20% in any relevant market.[427] If the market share of one or more parties to the agreement is not more than 20% at the time of entry into the agreement, and after the entry into force of the agreement is less than 25%, the exemption from the prohibition shall apply for a period of two consecutive calendar years following the year in which the 20% market share threshold was first exceeded.[428] If the market share of one or more parties to the agreement is not more than 20% at the time of entry into the agreement and exceeds 25% after the agreement enters into force, the exemption from the prohibition shall apply for a period of one calendar year following the year in which the market share initially exceeded the 25% threshold.[429]

452. In addition to the above conditions for block exemption, specialization agreements must also meet the four conditions for block exemption under Article 9 of the Competition Act (efficiency gains, fair share for consumers, the indispensability of the restrictions, and no elimination of competition). There is no provision for this condition in the Specialization BED, but it is derived from the general provisions of the Competition Act.

453. Block exemption does not apply to specialization agreements containing restrictions aimed at: (1) determining fixed or minimum prices when the product of specialization is sold to a third party; (2) limiting volume of production or sales; or (3) market or customer division.[430]

C. Standardization

454. Based on publicly released information and relevant Agency documents, there is no case law in cases of infringement related to standardization agreements.

455. Standardization agreements are not mentioned in the relevant decrees on the block exemptions of certain agreements from prohibition, nor are there adequate guidance for the evaluation of these agreements.

426. *Id.*, Art. 3.
427. *Id.*, Art. 5 para. 1.
428. *Id.*, Art. 5 para. 2.
429. *Id.*, Art. 5 para. 3.
430. *Id.*, Art. 4 para. 1.

D. Joint Production

456. Joint production agreements are regulated by the Specialization BED. According to the Specialization BED, a joint production agreement is an agreement between two or more contracting parties that aims to regulate the conditions of joint production.[431]

457. Based on the publicly released information and relevant Agency documents, there is no case law in cases of infringement related to joint production agreements.

E. Joint Purchasing

458. Joint purchasing agreements are not regulated by any of the block exemption decreases in relation to horizontal cooperation. In the case law of the Agency, there have been no cases of investigation of impairment of competition in the cases of joint purchasing agreements.

F. Joint Selling

459. In a certain way, joint participation in a tender can also be seen as joint selling, so we can say that there is a specific practice in cases of joint selling.

§2. VERTICAL AGREEMENTS

I. General Framework

460. A vertical restrictive agreement may be exempted from appropriate sanctions provided they meet the requirements of Vertical BED or if it obtains an individual exemption.

461. Vertical BED in Montenegro is harmonized with the relevant EU vertical block exemption regulation.[432] According to the Vertical BED, the block exemption applies to vertical agreements containing restrictions under Article 8 of the Competition Act, and in particular to: (1) exclusive distribution agreements; (2) selective distribution agreements; (3) agreements with the exclusivity clause; (4) commercial representation agreements without the agent's commercial risk; (5) franchising agreements. This is just an *exempli causa* list of vertical agreements that can benefit from a block exemption.[433]

---

431. *Id.*, Art. 2 para. 1 item 4.
432. Commission Regulation (EU) No. 330/2010 of 20 Apr. 2010 on the application of Art. 101(3) of the TFEU to categories of vertical agreements and concerted practices, O.J. [2010] L 102/1.
433. Vertical BED, Art. 3 para. 1.

462. The block exemption shall also apply to vertical agreements concluded between associations and members of associations, as well as between associations and suppliers of association members, provided that: (1) all members of the association are retailers selling contract products to end consumers, and (2) certain members of the association, together with related undertakings, do not have a total annual revenue of more than EUR 250,000, and (3) members of the association have a joint market share of less than 50% in the relevant market.[434]

463. The block exemption does not apply to agreements concluded between individual members of the association and to decisions of the association.[435] Unfortunately, according to publicly available information, the Agency has not investigated these cases so far.

464. Vertical agreements may be exempted from the prohibition when the parties' market share is less than 30%.[436] In the event that the market share of one or more participants to the vertical agreement increases above 30% in the period after the conclusion of the agreement and does not exceed 35%, the block exemption will also apply for a period of the next two consecutive calendar years following the year in which the 30% market share threshold was first exceeded.[437] The seller's market share is calculated on the basis of the seller's turnover in the total turnover of the relevant product, by value or volume, in the previous calendar year.[438] The buyer's market share is calculated on the basis of the volume of purchases made by the buyer in the total purchases of the relevant product, by value or volume, in the preceding calendar year.[439]

465. Block exemption does not apply to vertical agreements which contain hardcore restrictions regulated in Article 5 of the Vertical BED. These restrictions are a literal translation of the restrictions listed in Article 4 of the EU Vertical BED.

II. Distribution

A. Exclusive Distribution

466. Under the Vertical BED exclusive distribution agreement, the seller undertakes to sell the products subject to the agreement only to one distributor in a specific geographical area.[440]

467. In the practice of the Agency, there have been no cases of examining the potential illegality of an exclusive distribution agreement.

434. *Id.*, Art. 4 para. 1.
435. *Id.*, Art. 4 para. 2.
436. *Id.*, Art. 5 para. 1.
437. *Id.*, Art. 5 para. 3.
438. *Id.*, Art. 6 para. 1.
439. *Id.*, Art. 6 para. 1.
440. *Id.*, Art. 3 para. 1 item 1.

B. Exclusive Dealing

468. Exclusive purchasing agreements are regulated by Vertical BED. Vertical BED applies to agreements with an exclusivity clause and in particular a pre-emptive or exclusive purchase, exclusive sale or exclusive sale for a particular buyer or a group of buyers, under which: (a) seller undertakes to sell the product only to one buyer authorized to resell exclusively to a specific other customer or to a specific group of other customers; (b) the buyer undertakes, directly or indirectly, to procure the products subject to the agreement solely from one supplier for the purpose of production and/or sale; (c) the seller undertakes, directly or indirectly to sell the products subject to the agreement only to one buyer for the purpose of further production and/or sale.[441]

469. In the practice of the Agency, there have been no cases of examining the potential illegality of such agreements.

C. Selective Distribution

470. Selective distribution Agreements are covered by the Vertical BED. Vertical BED defines selective distribution agreement as an agreement obliging the seller to sell the products subject to the agreement exclusively to pre-selected buyers based on clear qualitative and/or quantitative criteria, whereby the buyer undertakes not to sell the contract product to other buyers outside the established seller's selective distribution network.[442]

471. In the practice of the Agency, there have been no cases of examining the potential illegality of selective distribution agreements.

D. Franchising

472. Vertical BED defines a franchise agreement as an agreement in which the franchisor provides the franchisee with the right to use the subject of the franchise for the purpose of producing and/or selling the object of the agreement, in return for financial or other compensation.[443]

473. In the practice of the Agency, there have been no cases of examining the potential illegality of the franchise agreement.

---

441. *Id.*, Art. 3 para. 1 item 3.
442. *Id.*, Art. 3 para. 1 item 2.
443. *Id.*, Art. 3 para. 1 item 5.

III. Technology Licensing

474. The Vertical BED provides that block exemption applies to vertical agreements that determine the transfer of intellectual property rights to the buyer, where the transfer of intellectual property rights is not an underlying subject of the agreement and is directly related to the use, sale or resale of the goods or services by the buyer.[444]

475. In addition to the above provision, Montenegro has a special decree on block exemption for technology transfer agreements (Transfer technology BED).

476. Transfer technology BED defines a technology transfer agreement as: (a) a contract between two independent undertakings for the purpose of manufacturing the contract product by the licensee and/or its subcontractors, or (b) the assignment of technological rights between two independent undertakings for the purpose of production of the contract product, and where part of the technology exploitation risk is borne by the licensor.[445]

477. In all cases of the conclusion of a technology transfer agreement, the condition for a block exemption is limited participation in the relevant market of the contracting parties. In the event of the conclusion of a technology transfer agreement between competitors in the market, the block exemption shall apply if the parties' joint market share in the relevant market does not exceed 20% in the relevant market. In the event that contracting parties are not competitors in the relevant market, the block exemption shall apply if each party's market share in the relevant market does not exceed 30% in the relevant market in which each party is engaged in economic activity.[446] In determining the market share, account shall be taken of the following: (1) the value of revenue generated (in the event that data on the value of revenue in the relevant market cannot be determined, the market share is determined on the basis of realized turnover); (2) data from the previous calendar year; (3) the realized value or volume of turnover of all contracting parties and its related undertakings.[447]

478. The block exemption does not apply to technology transfer agreements between competitors that establish restrictions that aim to: (1) limit the rights of one contracting party to independently determine the selling price to resellers; (2) limit the volume of production of the contract product; (3) divide customers or sale territory; (4) restrict the licensee right to use the licensee with his own technology or restrict the right of any contracting party to conduct research and development.[448]

---

444. *Id.*, Art. 3 para. 1 item 7.
445. Transfer technology BED, Art. 3 para. 1.
446. *Id.*, Art. 4 para. 2.
447. *Id.*, Art. 4 para. 3.
448. *Id.*, Art. 5 para. 1.

A. *Patent Licensing*

479. The patent licensing is covered by the above-mentioned Transfer technology BED. For the purpose of Transfer Technology BED, technology rights are know-how and all other intellectual property rights, including applications for registration of those rights, and in particular patents, models, designs and copyrights in computer software.[449]

480. The Patent Law regulates the terms of patent protection but does not contain any provisions relating to rules on the protection of competition.[450]

B. *Trademark Licensing*

481. The interpretation of Transfer technology BED implies that it also applies to trademark licensing. However, Montenegrin competition regulation does not contain specific rules regarding trademark licensing. In addition, in Montenegro, the registration procedure and the legal protection of trademarks are regulated by the Law on Trademarks.[451]

C. *Know-How and Trade Secret Licensing*

482. Know-How is covered by Transfer technology BED. For the purpose of Transfer Technology BED, know-how is a set of information, which is the product of experience, testing and application, and which are: (a) secret; (b) significant and useful for the production of the contract product; and (c) recognizable and clear.

483. Montenegrin competition regulation does not contain any special rules regarding trade secret licensing.

---

449. *Id.*, Art. 3 para. 1.
450. Law on Patents (*Zakon o patentima, Službeni list Crne Gore* 042/15, 002/17).
451. Trademark Law (*Zakon o žigu, Službeni list Crne Gore* 072/10, 044/12, 018/14, 040/16, 002/17).

Chapter 2. Dominant Undertakings' Prohibited Practices

484. Unlike cartel agreements where there were no instances of establishing their existence in the period of application of the former 2006 Competition Act until 2012, in a certain number of cases has been identified abuse of a dominant position. According to available data from the Agency's website, the first cases of establishing a dominant position were in 2011. In all of the proceedings, the then Administration for Protection of Competition acted at the request of the competition of the undertaking in a dominant position, not ex officio.

§1. Exploitative Practices

I. Excessive/Unfair Pricing

A. Javno Komunalno Preduzeće Nikšić

485. In 2011, Administration for Protection of Competition determined that the Public Utility Company, Komunalno Nikšić, had abused its dominant position in the relevant market of chapel rental services in the relevant geographical market of the municipality of Nikšić.[452] The abuse of a dominant position was carried out in such a way that the Price List of the funeral services of this company determined the higher price for the rent of the chapel for those users who did not buy funeral equipment from them. This restricts access to the use of the chapel by buyers of funeral equipment from other companies.

B. Simon Voyages

486. In 2011, Administration for Protection of Competition found that the company Simon Voyages from Berane had abused a dominant position in the relevant market of providing bus transportation services for primary and secondary school students.[453] This company had a dominant position on the basis of the Student Transportation Services Agreement, which was concluded with the Ministry of Education and Science. The abuse of a dominant position was carried out in a way that, in individually determined cases, a higher amount of the monthly fee was charged than the price determined by the said contract.

---

452. Agency Decision No. 01-UPI-49/49-11 of 15 Mar. 2011, available at (in Montenegrin): http://www.azzk.me/1/doc/zloupotrebe/JKP%20Komunalno%20Niksic.pdf (last accessed 11 Oct. 2019).
453. Agency Decision No. 01-UPI-1/39-11 of 6 May 2011, available at (in Montenegrin): http://www.azzk.me/1/doc/zloupotrebe/Simon%20Voyages.pdf (last accessed 11 Oct. 2019).

C. Vodovod Budva

487. The main activity of Vodovod i kanalizacija Budva (Water Supply and Sewerage Company) is the supply of drinking water to the citizens of Budva and the treatment and disposal of waste water. In the proceedings before the Agency, it was established that, by adopting the Decision on the Price of Water Supply and the treatment and disposal of waste water and the Decision on Fees for Utilities and Use and Maintenance of the Network, Vodovod Budva directly imposed an unjustifiably high price for the basic service by directly establishing a special monthly fee for maintaining and reading water meters in an inappropriately high amount of EUR 8,092. The obligation to pay a fee in this amount is conditioned as an additional obligation, which by its nature and purpose is not related to the subject matter of the principal service.

488. In 2015, the Agency initiated an investigation in the case of Vodovod Budva and prepared a sectorial analysis. During the sectorial analysis, it was found that the prices of water supply and the provision of municipal and other waste disposal services are significantly higher in the municipality of Budva compared to other municipalities in the coastal part of Montenegro, where the conditions of supply, economic opportunities of enterprises and citizens are similar.[454]

489. During the proceedings, the Agency determined that the market share of Vodovod Budva in the defined market is 100%, that there is no possibility of substitution of supply or demand and that the buyers have absolutely no possibility of changing suppliers regardless of the conditions. Following the proceedings, the Agency issued a decision declaring that Vodovod Budva engaged in the practice of abuse of a dominant position.[455] By the same decision, this company was ordered to prohibit further actions and within ninety days amend the Decision on fees for the provision of utilities and use and maintenance of the network. In the course of further activities, the Agency filed a petition for initiating misdemeanour proceedings with the competent Misdemeanour Court in Budva.[456]

490. Vodovod Budva filed a lawsuit with the Administrative Court to annul the Agency's decision.[457] The judgment of the Administrative Court of Montenegro rejected the lawsuit and rendered a decision that each party should bear their costs.[458] In addition, against the judgment of the Administrative Court, Vodovod

454. Agency's Annual Report for 2016, pp. 56–57.
455. Agency Decision No. 02-UPI-32/73-15 of 24 Mar. 2016. Available at (in Montenegrin): available at (in Montenegrin): http://www.azzk.me/1/doc/zloupotrebe/2016-03-24_zloupotreba_domin_polozaja%20Vodovod%20i%20kanalizacija%20Budva.pdf (last accessed 11 Oct. 2019).
456. *See* Part I, Ch. 5, §1, IV above.
457. *See* Part III, Ch. 4, §1 below.
458. Judgment of the Administrative Court No. 1097/2016 of 18 Jul. 2017, not available online.

Budva filed a request for reconsideration of a court decision with the Supreme Court of Montenegro.[459] The Supreme Court rejected the request for reconsideration of a court decision as unfounded.[460]

491. The rationale of the judgment of the Supreme Court states that Vodovod Budva indicates on no grounds that the Competition Act does not apply to the plaintiff, as it is established that he is an undertaking providing water supply services and performing an activity of public interest. Article 5 of the Competition Act stipulates that this law also applies to undertakings engaged in activities of public interest.[461]

D. Unfair Pricing Resolved by Commitments

492. During the investigation against LEDO Company, the Agency found that there was an impairment of competition in the form of abuse of a dominant position resulting from the application of different conditions to transactions of the same type with other undertakings, as well as the direct or indirect imposition of unjustified purchase or sale prices or other unjustified business conditions.

493. In 2015, in the process of monitoring and analysing the conditions of competition in the market for production and sale of ice cream and frozen food (fruits, vegetables, fish, meat, pastry dough, ready-made meals), the Agency collected data from undertakings in the retail market of the food products concerned on the sources and conditions of supply. The analysis and processing of the collected data determined the conditions for commercial cooperation between LEDO Podgorica Company and its related undertakings in the sales relationship in a retail channel to the largest buyers in the retail of food products in the territory of Montenegro. LEDO has put its buyers in an unequal position by applying different conditions to business transactions of the same kind with its buyers in the trade of the same product groups. During the investigation, LEDO submitted to the Agency, in accordance with Article 45, a proposal of measures, conditions and deadlines within which it would eliminate the negative effects of acting or failing to act. The Agency accepted the above acceptance of obligations and withdrew the petition for initiating misdemeanour proceedings with the Misdemeanour Court in Podgorica.[462]

II. Discrimination

494. In 2013, the Agency initiated a proceeding against the company RDC on suspicion of abuse of a dominant position in the market of providing access to the

459. Request for reconsideration of a court decision No. 1097/2016 of 18 Jul. 2017, not available online.
460. Judgment of the Supreme Court 415/17 of 19 Oct. 2017, not available online.
461. *See* Part I, Ch. 2, §3 above.
462. Agency's Annual Report for 2015, pp. 54–56.

necessary infrastructure and broadcasting signals for mobile telephony in the Montenegrin market. The proceeding was initiated with the aim of determining the justification for applying unequal conditions to the same transactions with different undertakings. More specifically, it was about applying different prices, contrary to the published price list of RDC, for three licensed mobile operators in Montenegro. This proceeding was discontinued in 2014 because there was no evidence that RDC had abused its dominant position in the relevant market.[463]

§2. Exclusionary Practices

I. Predation

495. In the practice of the Agency so far, there have been no cases concerning this type of prohibited activities.

II. Tying

496. In the practice of the Agency so far, there have been no cases concerning this type of prohibited activities.

III. Rebates

497. In the practice of the Agency so far, there have been no cases concerning this type of prohibited activities.

IV. Refusal to Deal

A. Luka Bar

498. One of the first serious cases of the application of competition law in Montenegro concerned the abuse of a dominant position by the Luka Bar. Luka Bar is a company the majority of which is owned by the state – whose main business activity is trans-shipment and storage of goods. Deciding upon the request of the company Jugopetrol Kotor from 17 June 2011, Administration for Protection of Competition issued a decision declaring that Luka Bar had abused its dominant position in the relevant market for the provision of services of trans-shipment of liquid cargo-petroleum products for transport by sea traffic in the relevant geographic market of Montenegro.[464] In this case, Luka Bar conditioned conclusion of the

463. Agency's Annual Report for 2013, p. 38.
464. Agency Decision No. 01-UPI-6/43-11 of 17 Jul. 2011, available at (in Montenegrin): http://www.azzk.me/1/doc/zloupotrebe/Luka%20Bar%20A.D.pdf (last accessed 11 Oct. 2019).

agreement with the company Jugopetrol Kotor, by accepting additional business obligations that were not related to the defined subject of the contract.

499. By the same decision, Administration for Protection of Competition ordered Luka Bar to submit to Jugopetrol AD Kotor and other service users an Agreement on determining mutual rights, obligations and responsibilities on market-acceptable obligations and without being conditioned with obligations not related to the subject matter of the contract.

500. The aforementioned decision of the Administration for Protection of Competition was annulled by the judgment of the Administrative Court. In the proceedings upon the lawsuit of Luka Bar, for Administrative Court it was not disputed that the Administration for Protection of Competition had determined that the Luka Bar AD had a dominant position on the Montenegrin market for the provision of services of trans-shipment of liquid cargo-petroleum products and transport by sea traffic. It was also undisputed that it had abused that position. It was disputable for the Administrative Court to determine measures against the participant. Namely, Article 42 of the 2006 Competition Act laid down in more detail the measures that the Administration for Protection of Competition may impose in the event of a dominant position being abused. However, the contested decision ordered measures that did not have grounds in Article 42, and no other regulation which envisaged those measures was given, which is why the contested decision could not be verified in that part.

501. In 2012, the Agency for the Protection of Competition, which was already established, virtually confirmed the earlier decision of the Administration for Protection of Competition that Luka Bar had committed an abuse of dominant position.[465] However, the entire Agency's decision has not been published on the Agency's website, so it is not possible to see what measures have been imposed on the company Luka Bar.

B. Jugopetrol Kotor AD

502. Jugopetrol Kotor AD is a petroleum company whose main activities are wholesale and retail of petroleum and petroleum products. Administration for Protection of Competition with its decision found that Jugopetrol Kotor had a dominant position in the relevant market for the provision of storage services of petroleum and petroleum products by a seaway in the narrower relevant geographical market of the territory Luka Bar.[466] It was also found that Jugopetrol AD Kotor

465. Agency Decision No. 01-UPI-6/43-11 of 24 Sep. 2012, available at (in Montenegrin): http://www.azzk.me/1/doc/zloupotrebe/Luka%20Bar%20A.D.pdf (last accessed 11 Oct. 2019).
466. Agency Decision No. 01-UPI-10/19-11 of 19 Jul. 2011, available at (in Montenegrin): http://www.azzk.me/1/doc/zloupotrebe/Jugopetrol.pdf (last accessed 11 Oct. 2019).

committed an act of abuse of a dominant position. It was determined that Jugopetrol AD Kotor had an obligation to transparently determine the conditions of business with potential users – lessees of storage facilities.

503. An administrative dispute was initiated before the Administrative Court against this Decision. After the proceedings, the Administrative Court annulled the Agency's Decision. In 2012, the Agency for the Protection of Competition, already formed at that time, corrected the omissions identified in the judgment of the Administrative Court No. 2634/11 of 30 May 2012, and literally confirmed the earlier Decision of the Administration for Protection of Competition that Jugopetrol AD Kotor had committed an act of abuse of a dominant position.[467]

C. Luka Kotor

504. In 2016, after the investigation, the Agency determined the abuse of dominant position undertaken by the Luka Kotor on the market for the provision of pilotage services within the relevant geographical market of the Bay of Kotor.[468] Luka Kotor is the operator of the seaport of Kotor. In this case, Luka Kotor for no reason refused to provide the agency BWA with the maritime infrastructure and thus prevented the motor yacht from entering the Luka Kotor because the agency had chosen Boka Pilot as a provider of pilotage services. During the proceedings, the Agency investigated whether Luka Kotor abused its dominant position by using its exclusive right as a concessionaire in the port of Kotor aquatorium (e.g., anchoring, berthing and related services) by requiring agents and ship operators to engage Luka Kotor also for pilotage services whenever Kotor was the arrival and departure port of a vessel.

505. The proceedings before the Agency established that Luka Kotor was providing pilotage services, but was not given the exclusive right to perform pilotage services within the entire Bay of Kotor, including the port of Kotor. In addition to Luka Kotor, two other entities are also authorized to provide pilotage services, issued by the competent Ministry. The Agency conducted an analysis of engaged pilotage services from three licensed business entities, where it was found that in more than 98% of cases the pilotage service in the port of Kotor aquatorium is performed by the Luka Kotor.[469]

506. The Agency's decision establishing the abuse of dominant position ordered Luka Kotor to establish non-discriminatory commercial conditions with potential port service users in a clear and transparent manner, by way of (1) informing the

467. Agency Decision No. 01-UPI-10/46-12 of 24 Sep. 2012, available at (in Montenegrin): http://www.azzk.me/1/doc/zloupotrebe/Jugopetrol%20II.pdf (last accessed 11 Oct. 2019).
468. Agency Decision No. 02-UPI-81/67-15 of 25 Oct. 2016, available at (in Montenegrin): http://www.azzk.me/1/doc/zloupotrebe/2016-10-25_Luka%20Kotor%20AD-zloupotr%20domin%20pol.pdf (last accessed 11 Oct. 2019).
469. Agency's Annual Report for 2016, pp. 57–58.

maritime agencies/ship operators of their right to independently and freely choose the providers of pilotage services in the port of Kotor; (2) informing the maritime agencies/ship operators that Luka Kotor does not have an exclusive right to provide pilotage service and that other services provided by Luka Kotor are not directly related to the pilotage service, especially in terms of contracting the terms and prices for the services in question separately and/or together with the pilotage service; (3) informing the Agency at least twice a year in the period of two years from the Agency's decision on the maritime agents' requests for of the pilotage service in the port of Kotor.

V. Price Squeeze

507. In the practice of the Agency so far, there have been no cases concerning these types of prohibited activities.

Chapter 3. Concentrations

508. Following an insight into the Annual Activity Reports, it can be seen that most of the Agency's obligations in the area of protection of competition relate to the process of concentration. Almost 100% of the approved concentrations in Montenegro were resolved in summary (fast-track) proceedings (without initiating proceedings).[470] Since its commencement, the Agency has approved 137 concentrations. Only in one case, the Agency has initiated an investigation on evaluation conditions of concentration (Phase II).

509. For example, in 2017, the Agency issued thirty-seven clearance decisions. All concentrations were resolved in a summary proceeding. In 2016, the Agency issued a total of twenty-eight clearance decisions.[471]

510. Out of the total of thirty-seven concentrations approved in fast-track (summary) proceedings in 2017, one was resolved by imposing additional measures, conditions and obligations that parties to the concentration must meet before or after the implementation of the concentration (in 2016, there was one concentration which required the imposition of additional measures, and in 2015 there were three concentrations which required the imposition of additional measures). In the structure of approved concentrations from 2017, one relates to the joint venture and thirty-six to control acquisition. Nine concentrations were conducted on the territory of Montenegro, while the remaining twenty-eight were extraterritorial. As regards the type of concentrations, seventeen horizontal, two vertical and nine conglomerate concentrations were approved.[472]

511. Concentrations for which requests are made are predominantly extraterritorial, they do not require carrying out of investigations and are dealt with in a summary proceeding. For concentrations taking place in the territory of Montenegro, it was not required to conduct investigations as it was found that they had no negative effects and that the concentration did not prevent, restrict and/or distort competition in the market.

512. In the event of imposing additional measures, conditions and obligations (*behavioural measures*) which must be implemented by the parties to the concentration before or after the implementation of the concentration, at least two conclusions should be drawn in the current practice of the Agency. First, the Agency does not often take the opportunity to impose additional measures, conditions and obligations. Second, the aforementioned possibility is used in summary proceedings.

513. The Agency publishes decisions on approved concentrations on its website. However, it published only the operative part of its decisions, without the statement of reasons. Therefore, it is not possible to carry out a detailed analysis and to

---

470. *See* Part III, Ch. 3, §2 below.
471. Agency's Annual Report 2016, pp. 50–51.
472. Agency's Annual Report 2017, pp. 50–51.

explain the Agency's practices in cases of issuing approval for concentrations. On the other hand, the Agency's Annual Reports mostly contain the statistical data on the number of concentrations implemented, their structure and the manner in which decisions on approval of the concentration were made. For this reason, in this part of the monograph, we will describe only approved concentrations with the imposition of additional measures and obligations, and a single concentration decided in the investigation (Phase II).

514. Finally, the Agency has not so far issued specific guidelines on the evaluation of concentration. In the Agency's Annual Reports, it was emphasized that in relation to this issue, the Agency also relies on applicable sources of EU law.

§1. Horizontal Mergers

515. In practice, horizontal mergers attract the most attention from the competent institutions. Nonetheless, the Agency has often approved horizontal merges in summary proceedings. When evaluating the effects of concentration in practice, the Agency starts from the market share and market structure.

I. Mercator/Solaris&Co

516. The concentration of participants, in this case, occurred in the relevant retail consumer goods market (consisting of retailing of food and non-food products) in the relevant geographical market of the Municipality of Ulcinj, resulted from the takeover of six Solaris & Co retail outlets (lease or sublease) by Mercator-CG, as well as certain equipment and supplies. This was the first time that the Agency approved concentrations with the imposition of additional obligations in the summary proceedings.

517. The Agency found in summary proceedings that the implementation of the concentration in question would not lead to prevention, restriction or distortion of effective competition in the Montenegrin market. However, considering the tendency of the possible increase of the market share of the acquirer, the Agency, in accordance with the provisions of Article 56 paragraph 1 item 4 of the Competition Act, ordered the company Mercator-CG to submit the following documents: (1) original or a certified copy of the Commercial Lease Agreement, Equipment Purchase Agreement and Stock Purchase Agreement, as well as (2) the Framework Agreement within fifteen days after its conclusion and (3) notify the Agency in writing of each future purchase, lease/sublease of retail outlets, as well as the opening of new outlets in the territory of the Municipality of Ulcinj.

II. Mercator/Kaća

518. In this case, it was a concentration of participants in the relevant retail consumer goods market consisting of retailing of food and non-food products in the relevant geographical market of the territory of the Municipality of Bar. Mercator-CG has leased four retail outlets, certain goods/ supplies, and kept a certain number of employees of the company Kaća from Bar. The Agency found in summary proceedings that the implementation of the concentration in question would not lead to the prevention, restriction or impairment of effective competition in the Montenegrin market. Similarly, the Agency ordered Mercator-CG d.o.o. Podgorica, Montenegro, to submit the original or certified copy of the Lease Agreement, as well as the Framework Agreement within fifteen days after its conclusion, and to inform the Agency in writing of any future purchase, lease/sublease of retail outlets, as well as the opening of new outlets in the Municipality of Bar that are over 200 m^2 in size.[473]

III. Grawe Osiguranje/Merkur Osiguranje

519. Concentration of undertakings on the market in this case resulting from the acquisition of individual control by the business entity Grawe osiguranje Podgorica (insurance company), over the joint-stock company Merkur osiguranje Podgorica (insurance company), by acquiring 100% of the share capital in the company in the market of life insurance on the territory of Montenegro. The Agency found in summary proceedings that the implementation of the concentration in question would not lead to the prevention, restriction or impairment of effective competition in the Montenegrin market, but considering the tendency of further growth of the market share of the acquirer, it ordered the acquirer to reports quarterly, within two years from issuing the Decision, on the following: (1) the number of concluded contracts /insurance policies; (2) market share in the total gross invoiced life insurance premium, and (3) takeovers, mergers, acquisitions, joint ventures and development or other business activities undertaken on the territory of Montenegro or outside the territory of Montenegro, but with effects on a defined relevant market.[474]

IV. Mercator/Klikovac

520. Concentration of undertakings by which Mercator-CG has leased three retail outlets Klikovac, Podgorica, Montenegro, for a period of ten years, engaged in retailing consumer goods consisting of retail sale of food and non-food products.[475]

473. Agency's Annual Report 2015, pp. 42–43.
474. Agency's Annual Report for 2016, p. 43.
475. Agency's Annual Report 2017, p. 63.

V. Telemach/M-Kabl

521. As practice has shown so far, the Agency has only in one case initiated an investigation and conditionally cleared the concentration.[476] The concentration was a result of the indirect acquisition of full control over M-cable by KKR & Co. L.P, registered in the United States, through its subsidiary United Group B.V, registered in the Netherlands and its Montenegrin subsidiary Telemach.

522. Based on the information available, the Agency, by its conclusion of 24 September 2015, initiated an investigation, which was conducted on the request for approval of the concentration, submitted by the Telemach Podgorica, which intended to gain complete control of the company M-Kabl Podgorica.

523. The parties to the concentration stated in their notification that they were present in the relevant market of Montenegro in the distribution of media content and the provision of internet access services, and that the telecommunications market, including the distribution of media content and the Internet, was extremely dynamic and changeable, and that competition between existing competitors was developed.

524. On the basis of the notification, the Agency has determined that the parties to the concentration are actual competitors in the narrow area of at least seven municipalities on the territory of Montenegro, and that the defined market is highly concentrated.

525. After conducting the investigation, the Agency issued a decision approving concentration with the imposition of the following additional measures, conditions and obligations (behavioural measures):

(1) Within forty-five days from the date of the implementation of the concentration, Telemach and its related undertakings KKR & Co. L.P. and United Group B.V. shall submit an offer to all existing cable operators distributing media content to end-users on the territory of Montenegro, to enter into a contract for the sale of audiovisual media content owned by the members of the group or for which the members of the KKR & Co. L.P. group have exclusive rights on the Montenegrin territory, under commercial terms agreed with the target company M-Kabl Podgorica or earlier with other buyers of the content in question.
(2) KKR & Co. L.P. group is obliged to conclude distribution contracts with the undertakings which will have accepted the offer referred to above and shall submit to the Agency a notarized copy of each such contract within three days from its conclusion.[477]

476. Agency Decision No. 02-UPI-75/3-15 of 24 Sep. 2015, not available online.
477. Agency Decision No. 02-UPI-75/36-15, not available online.

§2. Vertical Mergers

526. In the practice of the Agency, there have been no problematic cases of merger approvals and vertical merger cases. Like other types of mergers, the Agency has so far approved vertical mergers unconditionally in summary proceedings.

§3. Market/Product Extension Mergers

527. In the practice of the Agency so far, this type of mergers did not require increased attention of the Agency.

§4. Pure Conglomerate Mergers

528. In the practice of the Agency so far, pure conglomerate mergers did not require increased attention of the Agency.

§5. Joint Ventures

529. From the outset, the Agency did not have a significant number of joint ventures cases. For example, in 2017, the Agency approved a single concentration in the form of a joint venture.

Part III. Administrative Procedure

Chapter 1. Administrative Investigations Before the Antitrust Authority

§1. Initiative

I. General Sectors Enquiries

530. The Agency ex officio analyses the conditions of competition in deciding in each individual case of investigation for infringement of competition. However, the Agency may analyse the state of competition in a particular economic sector or analyse particular categories of agreements in different economic sectors (sectoral enquiries). The Agency has the power to conduct general sectoral enquiries, in cases when the price movements or other circumstances indicate the possibility of prevention, restriction or distortion of competition.[478]

531. Through the principle of sectoral analysis, multiple objectives are pursued to conduct competition policy. First, sectoral enquiries are the basis for the opinions and recommendations provided by the Agency to the competent state institutions, local government units, with the aim of eliminating barriers to market access. Second, the publication of research results strengthens the culture of protection of competition.

532. The Agency's powers in the process of conducting sectoral enquiries are broadly set by the Competition Act. In the process of conducting a sectoral analysis, the Agency may request from the undertakings to submit all necessary data and/or documents and may carry out any necessary research.[479] The Agency may request from the undertakings to supply all agreements, decisions, notices or data with a view to establishing the existence of the concerted practice. For example, agreements with customers, or, as the case may be, suppliers, as well as data on production or sale in the relevant period. Also, in the process of drafting a sectoral analysis, data may be requested by sector regulators, as well as data of undertakings which is a trade secret.

478. Competition Act, Art. 40 para. 1.
479. *Id.*, Art. 40 para. 2.

533. The results of a sectoral investigation must be publicly published. The Agency is obliged to post reports on sectoral enquiries carried out on its website.[480]

534. In its work to date, and especially in recent years, the Agency has conducted a considerable number of sectoral enquiries. Based on the available information, it can be seen that in the previous proceedings the Agency has carried out analyses in the following sectors: import, production and trade of milk and dairy products, soft drinks and promotional marketing billboards in the territory of several municipalities, analysis of supply and distribution of pharmaceutical products, analysis of the market for procurement of life and non-life insurance of public enterprises of Montenegro in public procurement procedures, the market of production and sale of ice cream and frozen food (fruits, vegetables, fish, meat, pastry dough, ready-made meals), water supply market in coastal municipalities, distribution of audiovisual media content on the territory of Montenegro and other sites – administrative municipalities in the territory of Montenegro.[481]

535. In addition, it should be noted that the preparation of sectoral enquiries requires the existence of human resources, as demonstrated by the experience and extensive analysis carried out by the European Commission. Given the lack of human resources, the current ability of the Agency to carry out sectoral analyses in a quality manner is put into question. Some of the enquiries were conducted in collaboration and with the support of EU-funded projects.[482]

II. Ex Officio Investigations

536. In accordance to the Competition Act, the Agency initiates the procedure for an investigation into impairment of competition ex officio and when it reasonably presumes the existence of impairment of competition on the grounds of submitted initiatives, information, documents and other available information.[483] The stated legal norm did not define precisely the manner of initiating the proceedings. Essentially, the proceedings for establishing impairment of competition are always initiated ex officio. Therefore, merely providing information or making a formal proposal from an interested third party to initiate the proceedings for establishing impairment of competition does not automatically imply an obligation on the Agency to initiate the proceedings.

537. Some lawyers argue that separation the *initiatives, information, documents and other available information*, as a special aspect of the initiation of proceedings, constitutes ambiguity and may create a problem in the interpretation of the norm.[484]

480. *Id.*, Art. 40 para. 4.
481. Agency's Annual Report, pp. 80–85.
482. *Id.*, p. 81.
483. Competition Act, Art. 28 para. 1.
484. Branka Lakočević & Gordana Pot, *Analiza zaštite konkurencije u Crnoj Gori* [*Analysis of Protection of Competition in Montenegro*], 4–5 (2016).

538. A party can initiate by its request the procedure in front of the Agency in two cases: (i) in proceedings for the issuance of the approval for implementation of a concentration, (ii) in the proceedings for an individual exemption.[485]

539. Status of a party to the proceedings before the Agency has: (1) an undertaking which filed a request for issuance of the approval for implementation of a concentration or the request for individual exemption of the agreement from prohibition, (2) an undertaking against whom the investigation has been initiated.[486]

540. The Competition Act explicitly states that the persons submitting initiative for an investigation into the impairment of competition, persons providing information, documents, data, professionals and other interested persons, organizations whose analyses are used in the proceedings, including also public bodies and organizations cooperating with the Agency during the proceedings, shall not have the status of the party in proceedings before Agency.[487]

III. Complaints

541. As we highlighted above, any natural or legal person may submit to the Agency an initiative to investigate an alleged infringement of competition, but without the status of a party to the proceedings.

542. The Competition Act does not have an explicit norm whether the complainant has certain procedural rights in the course of the investigation. For example, he has the right to be informed of the outcome of the initiative, etc. These rights have the origin from other regulations in Montenegro.

§2. Powers

I. Requests for Information

543. The Agency has the right to request information from the investigated party as well as from third parties. In fact, pursuant to Article 39 of the Competition Act, upon the request of the Agency, the undertakings and other legal and natural persons are obliged to supply data and documents relevant to establishing the facts in the proceedings before Agency.

544. Law prescribes that the deadline for submitting data and documents cannot be shorter than three nor longer than thirty days from the day of receiving the request.[488] Also, when carrying out an inspection in the undertaking's premises or

485. Competition Act, Art. 29.
486. *Id.*, Art. 27 para. 1.
487. *Id.*, Art. 27 para. 2.
488. *Id.*, Art. 39 para. 2.

taking a statement from the responsible persons in the legal person, the authorized person of the Agency may order that the documents and data be supplied within a set period of time.[489]

545. The undertaking who fails to comply with the request of the Agency to supply or communicate the required data is subject to a periodic fine.[490] For this situation, the Competition Act prescribes a fine in the amount from EUR 500 to EUR 5,000 for each day of non-compliance with the imposed obligations and up to 3% of aggregate turnover achieved in the financial year preceding the year in which the proceedings have been initiated.[491]

546. The person to whom the request was submitted shall not have the right to invoke a business secret as a reason for refusing to disclose certain data or to give documents.[492]

II. Investigating and Search Powers

547. Montenegrin competition law follows the best international practice in providing Agency with significant powers related to the collection of evidence relevant for the proceedings.

548. Necessary evidentiary actions with a view to properly establishing facts are taken in the investigation procedure. This includes, in particular, taking statements from the parties, witnesses, conducting expert examinations, obtaining data, documents and items, collecting information through inspection and temporarily seizing items.[493]

549. Investigation is conducted by the authorized persons of the Agency, designated by the Director of the Agency on a case-by-case basis.[494]

550. The Competition Act provides the Agency with wide-ranging powers of investigation when collecting information through inspection. If for the purpose of collecting information in the proceedings before the Agency it is necessary to conduct an inspection of business premises, land or vehicles of the party or another participant in the proceedings, the Director of the Agency shall adopt conclusion on conducting an inspection.[495] When conducting an inspection, the authorized person of the Agency has wide powers which *inter alia* includes the right to: (1) enter and inspect business premises, vehicles, land and other places where the party or another

489. *Id.*
490. *See* Part I, Ch. 5, §1, IV above.
491. Competition Act, Art. 60 para. 1 item 1.
492. *Id.*, Art. 39 para. 2.
493. *Id.*, Art. 31 para. 1.
494. *Id.*, Art. 31 para. 2.
495. *Id.*, Art. 32 para. 1.

undertaking engages in economic activities;[496] (2) examine business records and other documents;[497] (3) copy or scan business documentation and if that is not possible for technical reasons, to temporarily seize business documentation for the period necessary to make copies thereof;[498] (4) seal any business premises and business documents during the inspection to the extent necessary for the implementation thereof;[499] (5) take statements from the representative of the party or its employees, as well as the documents on the facts which relate to the subject matter of inspection and to make a record thereof, and if a written statement is necessary, to set the date by which such statement must be presented.[500]

551. The Competition Act does not regulate in detail the procedure for the conduct of an inspection. The Competition Act prescribes that the authorized persons of the Agency taking actions within the investigation have an official identification card, while other persons need to show special authorization to conduct an inspection in the procedure of gathering evidence.[501] The Director of the Agency is entitled to issue the official identification card and the authorization to conduct an inspection in the procedure of gathering evidence.[502]

552. If the holder of the premises or third party opposes the inspection, the assistance of the police can be secured. In order to involve the police in collecting information through inspection, two requirements need to be met. First, a formal request from the Agency. Second, police assistance is required just in specified circumstances – in the cases of obstructing or non-compliance with the orders of authorized persons. Upon fulfilment of this two conditions, the administration body competent for police affairs is obliged to provide assistance in the execution of certain actions in the proceedings and in particular in collecting information through inspection and temporarily seizing items in accordance with the law regulating powers and actions of the police.[503] Also, the person who is not a party to the proceedings is obliged to allow inspection if there is a reasonable suspicion that the economic activity or the items necessary for decision-making in the proceedings, is performed or are located in its buildings or premises.[504] However, it is not clear about consequences in a situation when they do not allow inspection. It is questioned whether this situation falls under periodic fine from Article 60 of the Competition Act because this article states that just *undertaking who fails to comply with the request of the Agency to supply or communicate required data is subject of a periodic fine.* Also, it is not clear how the Agency in this situation secure execution of the inspection. For example, whether the Agency needs to provide Court order or can just require the assistance of the police.

496. *Id.*, Art. 32 para. 2 item 1.
497. *Id.*, Art. 32 para. 2 item 2.
498. *Id.*, Art. 32 para. 2 item 3.
499. *Id.*, Art. 32 para. 2 item 4.
500. *Id.*, Art. 32 para. 2 item 5.
501. *Id.*, Art. 33 para. 1.
502. *Id.*, Art. 33 para. 2.
503. *Id.*, Art. 32 para. 3.
504. *Id.*, Art. 32 para. 2.

553. In relation to the investigation and search power of the Agency, it should be noted that the provisions of the Law on Administrative Procedure stipulate that the administrative activity of the Agency may restrict a party's right only if it is necessary to achieve a statutory purpose if this is proportionate to the objective to be achieved and does not violate human rights and freedoms.[505]

554. The Agency also has the power to perform dawn raids, or 'unannounced inspections', on the party's or third party's premises. Dawn raids in Montenegro have been very rarely carried out by the Agency in the past. However, in accordance with publicly available data in the last years have been executed several unannounced inspections. For example, in March 2017, the Agency carried out an unannounced inspection (dawn raid) at the business premises of Sava Trans Cetinje, a company engaged in freight transport, in order to collect data necessary for undertaking further actions. In April 2018, Agency publicly disclosed information that the Agency issued an unannounced insight into the business premises of the undertakings in the relevant market for the sale of electronic devices in the territory of Montenegro on the basis of the ex officio initiated procedure.[506]

555. Regardless of the fact that the Competition Act does not have an explicit norm, the Agency is obliged to ensure that all performed measures are proportionate to the pursued aims of the investigation and are time-limited.

556. In light of increasing activities of the Agency in performing dawn raids, it can be highlighted the question of the constitutionality of the Agency to perform dawn raids without a court order and especially in a situation when the holder of the premises or third party oppose the inspection. Constitution of Montenegro protect the privacy of premises and states that no one shall enter the dwelling place or other premises against the will of the possessor thereof and search them without a court warrant.[507] The search of premises shall be conducted in the presence of two witnesses. Competition law does not have an answer regarding the obligation of the Agency to request court order and which court is competent in this situation for issuance of the court order. Furthermore, the Constitution regulates the situation when an inspection can be made without the court order and the presence of witnesses. This can be done in three situation. First, if it is necessary for the prevention of execution of a criminal offence. Second, for immediate apprehension of a perpetrator. Third, in order to save people and property.[508] A suspicion of violation of competition law cannot be submitted to any of the three constitutional grounds for exemption from the rules under which the order of the court is necessary for the inspection of premises.[509]

505. Law on Administrative Procedure, Art. 6 para. 1.
506. *See* website of the Agency (available in English): http://www.azzk.me/jml/index.php/en/ (last accessed 11 Oct. 2019).
507. Constitution of Montenegro, Art. 41 para. 1.
508. *Id.*, Art. 41 para. 3.
509. *See* https://bdkadvokati.com/unconstitutionality-of-dawn-raids-in-the-competition-law-investigations-in-serbia-and-montenegro/ (last accessed 11 Oct. 2019).

III. Cooperation with Other State Institutions

557. The Agency cooperates with other state institutions in various ways (for the purpose of conducting an investigation, in the process of preparation of legislation, in the course of activities of sectoral analyses, etc.).

558. The Competition Act explicitly provides that the Agency has the power to conduct administrative procedure and take decisions in individual administrative matters.[510] In this sense, in addition to the laws and by-laws regulating the area of competition law and the powers of the Agency, the Law on Administrative Procedure applies to all actions and activities of the Agency. The Law on Administrative Procedure contains the general norm that public bodies are obliged to provide each other with legal assistance in administrative proceedings.[511] A public body may seek legal assistance when it needs knowledge of facts, data or other evidence available to another public body or when it is necessary to take action outside the area of a competent public body.[512] The public body which was asked for legal assistance is obliged to render such assistance without delay, within fifteen days from the day the assistance was requested at the latest.[513]

559. The Competition Act contains similar provisions. The Agency may request information from other state bodies and organizations, for the purpose of conducting proceedings. The Competition Act prescribes that public bodies, state administration bodies, local administration bodies, local self-government bodies and other legal persons, exercising public powers, are obliged to provide, on the request from the Agency, all data necessary in the process of decision-making by the Agency.[514] They are obliged to provide data which may constitute business secret, as well as other confidential data. Also, the deadline for submitting data to the Agency is fifteen days from the day of submitting the request. In case of denying, late or incomplete delivery of data which are important for conducting proceedings, the Agency may inform the authority supervising the operation of the obliged and/or request taking of necessary measures with a view to collecting the requested data.[515]

560. The Law on Administrative Procedure provides the possibility of international legal assistance and provides the procedure for its implementation. Legal assistance in relation to foreign authorities is provided in accordance with a valid international treaty, and in the absence of such a treaty, the principle of reciprocity

510. Competition Act, Art. 19 para. 3 item 19.
511. Law on Administrative Procedure (*Zakon o upravnom postupku, Službeni list Crne Gore* 056/14, 020/15 040/16 and 037/17).
512. *Id.*, Art. 44 para. 2.
513. *Id.*, Art. 44 para. 3.
514. Competition Act, Art. 37 para. 1.
515. *Id.*, Art. 37 para. 3.

applies.[516] If international treaties do not provide for the possibility of direct communication with foreign bodies, public bodies shall communicate with foreign institutions through the state administration bodies responsible for foreign affairs.[517]

561. Upon the request of the Agency, the police will provide assistance, in particular with respect to inspection collecting information through inspection.[518]

562. Legal assistance for performing certain actions in administrative proceedings may also be sought from the court. In accordance with the Law on Administrative Procedure, the Agency may ask the court to provide it with the documents necessary for conducting the administrative proceedings. The court is obliged to act on this request if this does not interfere with the court proceedings. The court may set a time limit for the Agency to return the files.[519]

563. The Agency cooperates with sector regulators in various areas, which is explained in a separate part of the monograph.[520]

564. The Agency cooperates with other state bodies in the field of competition and State aid. The Agency has signed cooperation protocols with almost all sectorial regulators, the Agency for Business Registers, the Faculty of Economics, the Ministry of the Interior etc.

§3. Right of Defence

I. Content and Notification of Opening Decisions

565. The Law on Administrative Procedure stipulates that the authorized official person conducts administrative procedure and issues the decision, as determined by the act on internal organization and systematization of the Agency.[521]

566. Formally, the procedure for investigation is initiated by the conclusion adopted by the Director.[522] The Competition Act prescribes mandatory content of the conclusion on initiating the proceedings. This legal act needs to contain the following elements: (1) description of the practices or acts that may constitute an impairment of competition;[523] (2) reasons and legal basis for initiating the proceedings;[524] (3) invitation to all natural and legal persons to submit to the Agency data, documents or information that may be relevant for proper and full determination of

516. Law on Administrative Procedure, Art. 45 para. 1.
517. *Id.*, Art. 45 para. 3.
518. Competition Act, Art. 32 para. 4.
519. Law on Administrative Procedure, Art. 44 para. 1.
520. *See* Part I, Ch. 2, §2 above.
521. Law on Administrative Procedure, Art. 46 para. 1.
522. Competition Act, Art. 28 para. 2.
523. *Id.*, Art. 28 para. 4 item 1.
524. *Id.*, Art. 28 para. 4 item 2.

facts in the proceedings.[525] The conclusion on initiating the proceedings is published in the Official Gazette of Montenegro and on the website of the Agency.

567. Proceedings shall be deemed initiated on the date of service on the party of the conclusion on initiating the proceedings.[526] The Competition Act does not contain detailed provisions regarding service. In this case, as in all other cases where a specific issue is not regulated by the Competition Act, provision of the Law on Administrative Procedure apply.

568. Service of documents is, as a rule, performed at the residence, office or workplace of the person to whom the document is being served, and to the lawyer at his law office.[527] Service of documents is performed on weekdays from 8.00 to 20.00.[528]

569. The service is confirmed by the certificate of delivery (delivery note), which contains the signature of the recipient and the delivery person, information on the document being delivered, as well as the date of delivery.[529] If the recipient is not found at the address at which the delivery was to be made, the delivery person will retry the delivery within twenty-four to seventy-two hours of the first attempt. If the delivery person failed to find the recipient in the second delivery attempt or refused to receive the document, the delivery person will make a written note thereof.[530] In this case, the delivery person leaves a notice of the premises where the document can be picked up as well as the date the notice was drawn up.[531] It shall be deemed that the service has been effectuated seven days from the date of this notice.[532]

570. In cases where personal delivery is not required, and the person to whom the delivery is to be made is not found in his residence, the delivery is made by serving the document on one of the adult members of his household.[533] If the delivery is made in the business premises, or at the workplace of the person to whom the document is to be delivered, and that person is not found there, the delivery can be made to the person employed in the same place if that person agrees to receive the document.[534] The service of process to an attorney may also be effectuated by giving the documents to a person employed in the law firm.[535]

---

525. *Id.*, Art. 28 para. 4 item 3.
526. *Id.*, Art. 28 para. 3.
527. Law on Administrative Procedure, Art. 72 para. 1.
528. *Id.*, Art. 73 para. 1.
529. *Id.*, Art. 84 para. 3.
530. *Id.*, Art. 84 para. 4.
531. *Id.*, Art. 84 para. 5.
532. *Id.*, Art. 84 para. 6.
533. *Id.*, Art. 85 para. 1.
534. *Id.*, Art. 85 para. 2.
535. *Id.*, Art. 85 para. 3.

571. In case that service cannot be made in accordance with the above rules, the service of process will be deemed effectuated within ten days of its publication on the Agency's website or bulletin board unless a longer period is specified by the Agency.[536]

572. In the proceedings against undertakings considered to be connected undertakings, service on one undertaking shall be deemed to be service on all connected undertakings.[537]

II. The Proceedings: Hearings, Access to File, Briefs

A. Hearings

573. In proceedings before the Agency, most of the persons against whom an investigation for infringement of competition has been initiated, decide to hire lawyers. Pursuant to the Law on Administrative Procedure, a party, or its legal representative, may appoint a lawyer or other legally qualified person to represent him/her in the proceedings as his/her proxy, except in cases where the party itself is required to make statements.[538] A power of attorney may be made in writing or given orally on the record. If the power of attorney is made in writing and the Agency questions its veracity, it will ask for a certified power of attorney.[539] The content of the power of attorney is relevant to the scope of the power of attorney. The power of attorney can be given for the whole administrative procedure or only for certain actions in the procedure, and it can be limited in time.[540]

574. The authorized officer independently determines the facts and circumstances in the administrative procedure and decides on the administrative matter on the basis of the established facts and circumstances.[541] What facts and circumstances will be taken as evidence shall be determined by authorized officer by a free evaluation, on the evaluations of each evidence separately and of all the evidence together, as well as on the basis of the results of the entire administrative procedure.[542]

575. The general rule set in the Competition Act is that the Agency shall decide without holding an oral hearing unless it finds on a reasoned request from the party or at its own discretion during the proceedings that it is necessary to hold an oral hearing.[543] Law on Administrative Procedure, applies to the issues in relation to hearings, since this question is not in detailed regulated by the Competition act.

536. *Id.*, Art. 85 para. 2.
537. Competition Act, Art. 41.
538. Law on Administrative Procedure, Art. 56 para. 1.
539. *Id.*, Art. 56 para. 2.
540. *Id.*, Art. 56 para. 3.
541. *Id.*, Art. 12 para. 1.
542. *Id.*, Art. 12 para. 2.
543. Competition Act, Art. 36 para. 1.

576. Law on Administrative Procedure provides that a record shall be drawn up of the oral hearing. The record shall include the name of the public body, place, day and time, administrative matter concerning the administrative proceedings, first name and last name of the authorized officer, the parties present and their representatives, proxies or representatives of third parties, a brief and accurate description of the course of the oral hearing, the contents of the actions carried out and the statements given in the administrative procedure, as well as information on the documents used in the administrative procedure.[544]

577. The record will be read to the parties before the conclusion. At the end of the record, it will be stated that the record has been read and that no objections have been made or, if objections have been made, their contents will be briefly stated. The record shall be signed by the authorized officer and the court reporter if any.[545] The record is evidence of the course and content of the oral hearing and has the legal force of a public document.[546]

578. The proceedings before the Agency in which an oral hearing is held is closed to the public.[547]

B. Inspection of the File

579. The Agency is obliged to enable the parties to examine the file and to inform them of the course of the proceedings.[548]

580. The party has the right to examine the case files, make the necessary notes and obtain copies of the file at his own expense. Reviewing case files is free of charge and is carried out under the supervision of an authorized officer.[549] The request to review case files and obtain copies of those files may be made in writing, orally, or electronically.[550]

581. The Agency shall, within five days from the date of submitting the request for reviewing of case files, provide conditions for reviewing of case files and obtaining copies.[551]

544. Law on Administrative Procedure, Art. 65 para. 2.
545. *Id.*, Art. 65 para. 3.
546. *Id.*, Art. 66.
547. Competition Act, Art. 36 para. 2.
548. Law on Administrative Procedure, Art. 16.
549. *Id.*, Art. 68 para. 1.
550. *Id.*, Art. 68 para. 2.
551. *Id.*, Art. 68 para. 3.

C. Briefs

582. During the proceedings, parties have the right to submit written briefs to the Agency. This question is in detailed regulated by the Law on Administrative Procedure.

583. Briefs must be sufficiently clear. In order to act upon it, it must include the following: the name of the Agency; the subject matter of the brief; first and last name, permanent or temporary residence and address, or name and seat of the party, first and last name of the attorney, proxy or representative, as well as the manner in which the party wants the Agency to respond to the brief.[552]

584. A party may submit a brief to the Agency by direct submission, submission by post, fax or electronically.[553]

585. If the submission contains a formal deficiency, or if the submission is unintelligible or incomplete, an authorized officer of the Agency shall, within than three days following the day of the receipt of the brief, request the submitter to eliminate the deficiencies and determine a deadline for the submitter to do so.[554] If the submitter eliminates the deficiencies within the specified time limit, the brief shall be regarded as duly submitted from the beginning.[555] Otherwise, the Agency will reject the brief.

586. At the request of a party, the Agency shall issue a certificate stating that the brief has been received, as well as the date and time of receipt, the subject of the brief and, if any, the list of documents submitted with the brief. There is no fee for issuing the certificate.[556]

587. A brief shall be regarded to have been submitted within the deadline if it was submitted to the Agency before the expiry of the deadline.[557] If a deadline-bound brief is submitted to a non-competent authority before the deadline expires and is received by the Agency after the deadline, it shall be regarded to have been submitted within the deadline.[558] When the brief is filed by registered mail or telegraph, the day of submission to the postal operator shall be considered as the day of submission to the Agency.[559]

---

552. *Id.*, Art. 59 para. 2.
553. *Id.*, Art. 59 para. 3.
554. *Id.*, Art. 60 para. 1.
555. *Id.*, Art. 60 para. 2.
556. *Id.*, Art. 64 para. 2.
557. *Id.*, Art. 90 para. 1.
558. *Id.*, Art. 90 para. 2.
559. *Id.*, Art. 90 para. 3.

D. Protected Data and Privileged Communication

588. The Agency has the right to impose a measure of protection of the source of information or specific information (protected information). Status of protected information can be granted ex officio or by request of the authorized person. The Competition Act in detailed regulates the procedure for imposing this measure in both situations.

589. Three conditions need to be met in order to adopt the status of protected information. First, request for adopting the status of protected information could be submitted by the person who submitted the initiative for investigating impairment of competition or a third person who submitted and/or made available the requested information in the proceedings. Second, the Agency will adopt request, if it assesses that the request of the applicant is justified and more important than the need to inform the public of the subject of such request.[560] Third, the person who requests the status of protected information is obliged to demonstrate that it is likely that the damage will arise from disclosing the source of information and/or the content of the information the request relates to.[561]

590. The Agency may stipulate that certain information has the status of protected information ex officio when it deems that data protection is necessary to protect the interests of the applicant for the infringement of competition or of the person who disclosed the information in the procedure.[562]

591. The conclusion on the protected of information is adopted by the Director of the Agency.[563] Protected information shall not have the status of information of public importance within the meaning of the law regulating free access to information of public importance.[564]

592. Client-attorney communication directly relating to the proceedings is treated as privileged communication.[565] Privileged communication is confidential and may not be used as evidence in the proceedings.[566]

593. If the abuse of privileged communication is suspected, the Agency may examine its content and/or adopt a conclusion on not recognizing communication as privileged. The law does not in detailed specify what can be considered as abuse in this context.[567]

---

560. Competition Act, Art. 38 para. 1.
561. *Id.*, Art. 38 para. 2.
562. *Id.*, Art. 38 para. 3.
563. *Id.*, Art. 38 para. 4.
564. *Id.*, Art. 38 para. 5.
565. *Id.*, Art. 34 para. 1.
566. *Id.*, Art. 34 para. 2.
567. *Id.*, Art. 34 para. 3.

594. Law on Attorneys regulates the status of privileged communication between attorney and client.[568]

595. The lawyer is obliged to keep secret all the information obtained in the provision of legal assistance. Employees who work or have worked with a lawyer also have this obligation.[569] Also, documents and information obtained during the search of a lawyer and a law firm cannot be used to conduct proceedings against any party of that law firm.[570]

III. Statement of Objections

596. Before it makes a final decision, the Agency shall be obliged to deliver to all the parties against whom the proceedings have been initiated a written notice of established facts, circumstances and conclusions in the proceedings.[571]

597. The party against whom the proceedings have been initiated shall have the right to complain against the statement of objection, within a period which may not be shorter than fifteen days from the day of receiving the notice.[572] In the statement of objections, the Agency set a deadline for a response.

598. In its complaint, the party may propose hearing additional witnesses and presenting supplementary evidence.[573]

IV. Final Hearing and Decision

A. *Final Hearing*

599. The Competition Act sets out as a general rule that the Agency shall decide without holding an oral hearing. Throughout the procedure, the Agency may take statements from all persons who may have direct and indirect knowledge of the procedure itself, as well as of the conditions of competition in the market and other facts that may be helpful in the decision-making process. The Law on Administrative Procedure provides that any means suitable for establishing the facts which are appropriate to the particular case, such as documents, statements of witnesses, statements of parties, findings and opinions of expert witnesses, interpreters and inspection, may be used as evidence.[574] Common facts and facts known to the Agency need not be proven.

568. Law on Attorneys (*Zakon o advokaturi, Službeni list Crne* Gore 073/10, 022/17).
569. *Id.*, Art. 10 para. 4.
570. *Id.*, Art. 23 para. 6.
571. Competition Act, Art. 35 para. 1.
572. *Id.*, Art. 35 para. 2.
573. *Id.*, Art. 35 para. 3.
574. Law on Administrative Procedure, Art. 107 para. 1.

600. The oral hearing shall be convened and held at the proposal of the official conducting the proceedings and shall be held regularly in proceedings with parties with opposite interests and in any case in which one of the parties to the proceedings proposes to hold an oral hearing. Oral hearings may also be held to hear witnesses or expert witnesses, in which case all parties to the proceedings may ask questions to witnesses and expert witnesses in order to resolve the disputed facts.

B. Decision

601. As already noted above, the rules of administrative procedure apply in proceedings before the Agency, except where certain rules for conducting administrative proceedings are directly prescribed by the Competition Act. During the procedure, the Agency may make different decisions. The Agency may: (1) determine the violation of the law and issue a decision establishing the violation, order the measures that an undertaking must take and initiate misdemeanour proceedings before a competent misdemeanour court; (2) order implementation of interim measures; (3) suspend proceedings initiated ex officio or at the request and at the proposal of the person concerned, if it finds that, based on all established facts, the law could not have been violated, or if the party against whom the proceedings were conducted adopted the measures, deadlines and conditions necessary to establish effective competition in the market.

602. The Agency renders the ultimate decision on the merits in the form of a decision. When the Agency finds that an agreement prevents, restricts or distorts competition in the relevant market, it shall prohibit the enforcement of such agreement by means of decision.[575] Also, by this decision, the Agency shall order the parties to the proceedings to fulfil specific conditions or take specific measures, i.e., behavioural and structural measures proportionate to the infringement committed, as well as the time limits for the performance thereof.[576]

603. When the Agency finds the abuse of dominant position, it shall by means of resolution: (1) establish the dominant position of an undertaking as well as the duration of the abusive practice,[577] (2) prohibit the parties to the proceedings practices and actions abusing dominant position,[578] and (3) order behavioural and structural measures and time limits for their implementation.[579]

604. The Law on Administrative Procedure stipulates a decision in the administrative procedure shall be issued within thirty days from the day of initiating the procedure unless otherwise stipulated by a special law.[580]

---

575. Competition Act, Art. 42 para. 1.
576. *Id.*, Art. 42 para. 2.
577. *Id.*, Art. 43 para. 1 item 1.
578. *Id.*, Art. 43 para. 1 item 2.
579. *Id.*, Art. 43 para. 1 item 3.
580. Law on Administrative Procedure, Art. 114.

605. The Competition Act sets time limits for adopting resolutions on establishing an infringement of competition, which are exempted from general deadlines for the adoption of the resolution which is prescribed by the Law on General Administrative Procedure. The Agency is obliged to adopt the resolutions establishing an infringement of competition within twenty-four months from the day of service of the conclusion on initiating proceedings.[581] This deadline can be additionally extended for maximum twenty-four months if the decision has not been adopted for justified reasons within twenty-four months from the day of service of the conclusion on initiating proceedings.[582] If the Agency fails to adopt a resolution within the prescribed time, the proceedings are discontinued.

606. The Law on Administrative Procedure stipulates that the administrative procedure must be conducted without delay and with minimum expenses, but in a manner that all the facts and circumstances relevant for the successful and complete exercise and protection of the rights and legal interests of the parties are properly and completely established.[583] In the practice of the Agency, there are cases of a deliberate delay in proceedings initiated by parties through the exercise of the rights conferred on them by the Law on Administrative Procedure. One of the possible ways is through initiating a request for exemption of an official. Pursuant to the Law on Administrative Procedure, an official shall be exempted if: (1) he/she is the party, witness, expert witness, proxy or legal representative of the party to the proceedings concerned; (2) he/she is related to the party, representative or proxy in direct blood kinship or side-line kinship up to the fourth degree of kinship, inclusive, or if he or she is the spouse or out of wedlock partner; (3) he/she has a family relationship with the party, its representative or proxy, or is a guardian, adoptive parent, adoptive child or foster parent; (4) he/she has already participated in the first instance procedure; (5) he/she is in interest, contractual or other relationship with the party on the basis of which he/she receives compensation or other income, or is a member of the board of directors, supervisory board or other working or professional body of the party; (6) may benefit or harm the outcome of the administrative proceedings; (7) there are other circumstances which cast doubt on his impartiality.[584] The Director of the Agency shall decide on the exemption of the official.

607. The operative part of the resolutions establishing an infringement of competition is published in the Official Gazette and on the website of the Agency.[585] The Agency may request the undertaking to submit a report on the compliance with obligations, measures, conditions and time limits ordered by a resolution.[586]

581. Competition Act, Art. 62 para. 1.
582. *Id.*, Art. 62 para. 2.
583. Law on Administrative Procedure, Art. 10.
584. *Id.*, Art. 48 para. 1.
585. Competition Act, Art. 61.
586. *Id.*, Art. 63.

Chapter 2. Voluntary Notifications and Clearance Decisions

§1. Individual Exemption

608. In cases where undertakings are unable to determine the fulfilment of the conditions for exemption of restrictive agreement, they have the opportunity to file an agreement with all the evidence and facts in the assessment of the fulfilment of conditions for an individual exemption.

609. An individual exemption from the prohibition of a restrictive agreement in Montenegrin Competition law is possible, after fulfilment of the condition set in the Competition Act. In Article 9 of the Competition Act, it is prescribed that restrictive agreements may be exempted from the prohibition if: (1) they contribute to improving the production or distribution of goods or services, or to promoting technical or economic progress, (2) while allowing consumers a fair share of the resulting benefit in the relevant market, (3) provided that they impose only restrictions which are indispensable to the attainment of objectives of the agreements, and (4) do not afford such undertakings the possibility of eliminating competition in the relevant market or a substantial part thereof.

610. On the request from a party to the agreement for an individual exemption, the Agency shall approve an individual exemption if the agreement fulfils the conditions laid down in Article 9 of the Competition Act.[587] The burden of proof that the four general conditions referred to in Article 9 of the Competition Act have been fulfilled lies on applicant.[588]

611. The content and the manner of submitting the request for individual exemption is prescribed by the Ministry in Rulebook on the content of the request for individual exemptions. Parties to the agreement jointly submit the application, and the party to the agreement whose registered office is in the territory of Montenegro, i.e., which directly or indirectly participates in turnover in the territory of Montenegro submit the application independently.[589] The applicants are obliged to submit to the Agency a detailed list of data which are significant for the evaluation of the fulfilment of conditions for an individual exemption. This, *inter alia*, includes the following documents and information: (i) name, registered office, scope of business of all participants to the agreement, and the extract from the Central Register of Business Entities for all participants to the agreement and related persons, who directly or indirectly perform turnover in the territory of Montenegro; (ii) the description of the market where participants to the agreement conduct their business, and information regarding the markets where the effects of the agreement are anticipated with particularly information regarding: (a) characteristics and structure of the relevant

587. Competition Act, Art. 12 para. 1.
588. *Id.*, Art. 12 para. 2.
589. Rulebook on content of the request for individual exemptions, Art. 2 para. 1.

market and market shares of the market participants; (b) characteristics and structure of vertically connected, complement and close markets with detailed description of systems of production, turnover, sale and distribution of products and market shares of the market participants; (c) market position of participants to the agreement and their economic and financial strength; (d) description of actual and potential competition and their business; (e) legal and other obstacles for entering the relevant market; (f) scope of the actual purchasers' demand for relevant product and assessment of possibility of procurement from other sources; (iii) clarification of economic benefits which are direct consequence of the agreement; (iv) clarification of overall effect the agreement has on consumers and development of competition at relevant market.[590] The applicants can file other data they consider potentially significant for the evaluation of the fulfilment of conditions for an individual exemption.

612. If the foreseen conditions are met, the Agency issues an administrative act granting exemption from the prohibition of restrictive agreement.

613. The Competition Act does not contain a provision on the deadline for granting a decision on exemption of individual agreement on prohibition. After reviewing the approved decisions available on the Agency's website, it was noted that the deadline is five years. In addition, the Law does not contain provisions on the possibility of extending the deadline to a certain period of time.

614. In its Annual Report the Agency noted that, in its assessment, it applies criteria arising from the application of the competition rules applicable in the EU, in particular from Articles 101 of the TFEU and interpretative instruments adopted by the EU institutions.

615. In accordance with the Agency's Tariff, the application for individual exemptions is subject to a fee in the amount of EUR 1,000.

616. This institute is not used often in the practice of work of Agency in Montenegro. For example, in the Agency's Annual Report for 2016, there was no information regarding using this institute (we suppose it was not used in this period). However, there were two cases in 2017 and two cases in 2018.[591]

---

590. *Id.*, Art. 3 para. 1.

591. In the first case of individual exemption in 2017, the Agency issued a Decision granting an individual exemption from the prohibition of the Agreement on essential elements of future cooperation between Bavaria N.V. Holand and its related undertakings Apatinska pivara, Industrija piva i sokova Trebjesa Nikšić, Zagrebačka pivovara and Molson Coors, Banja Luka, Republika Srpska, Bosna i Hercegovina. The exemption is granted for a period of five years from the date of conclusion of the Agreement. In the second case, the Agency issued a Decision granting an individual exemption from the prohibition of the Distribution Agreement concluded between Phillip Morris Operations Niš, Serbia and Neregelia Podgorica, Montenegro. The exemption is granted for a period of five years from the date of conclusion of the Agreement. Agency's Annual Report for 2017, pp. 41–42.

§2. NEGATIVE CLEARANCE

617. It is not possible to a party of a restrictive agreement to request and obtain from the Agency formal decision confirming that the agreement is not prohibited. However, the parties may ask for an opinion from the Agency on the legality of the Agreement or its particular provision. Request for obtaining the Opinion from the Agency needs to be made in advance, before concluding the agreement in order not to be at risk to be declared null and void.

618. The opinion of the Agency does not have the power of administrative act but has certain legal value for the applicant. In the Agency's Annual Report for 2017, there were no requests from the parties to the Agency for issuing this type of opinion.

Chapter 3. Merger Control

§1. Preliminary Filing Obligations

I. Criteria and Thresholds

619. In accordance with the Competition Act, the concentration in Montenegro is implemented only on the basis of the approval, which is issued by the Agency upon the request of the undertakings.[592] An undertaking is required to notify the Agency of each intent to enforce a concentration if either of the two conditions is met:

(1) the combined aggregate annual turnover of at least two parties to the concentration achieved in the market of Montenegro exceeds EUR 5 million in the preceding financial year; or
(2) the combined aggregate annual worldwide turnover of the parties to the concentration achieved in the preceding financial year exceeds EUR 20 million if at least one party to the concentration achieved EUR 1 million in the territory of Montenegro in the same period.[593]

Intra-group turnover of the parties to the concentration shall not be taken into account when calculating the combined aggregate annual turnover.[594]

620. In cases of non-compliance with the notification of the intended concentration within the time limits provided by the Law, the Agency shall punish the acquirer of the control with an adequate fine.

621. The Agency does not evaluate all business transactions that have the characteristics of concentration, but only those significant economic forces, which are observed through the total revenues of the undertakings in the year preceding the concentration. In case that concentration is implemented, the Agency may order the parties to the concentration to submit the request for issuance of the approval for implementation of a concentration if their combined market share in the relevant market of Montenegro exceeds 60%. The burden of proof of the combined market share of the parties to the concentration shall lie with the Agency.[595] Based on the publicly available information, the Agency has not used this authority. Only exceptionally, the Agency may initiate a concentration assessment ex officio – in cases where the undertakings do not report the concentration, in the case of abolition or modification of the issued decision on concentration, or in the case of determining measures after the implementation of the prohibited concentration.

---

592. Competition Act, Art. 50 para. 1.
593. *Id.*, Art. 50 para. 2.
594. *Id.*, Art. 50 para. 5.
595. *Id.*, Art. 50 para. 4.

622. The procedure for issuance of the approval for implementation of a concentration is initiated on the basis of the request of the party to be submitted to the Agency. Where thresholds are met, a notification must be submitted to the Agency within fifteen days from the earlier of:

(1) conclusion of the agreement or contract representing the basis for the concentration;
(2) announcement of the public call, or bid or closing of the public bid, or
(3) the acquisition of control.[596]

623. A notification can also be submitted in advance, based on a demonstration of a serious intent to effect a concentration. The Competition Act prescribes that such an event can be, for example, signing a letter of intent, announcing the intention to make a bid or another manner preceding a request of the party.[597]

624. When the control over the whole or parts of one or more undertakings is acquired by another undertaking, the request shall be submitted by the undertaking acquiring the control. In case of a joint venture, all undertakings concerned shall submit a joint request.[598]

625. The content and the manner of submitting a request for issuance of the approval for implementation of concentration is prescribed in more detail by Guidance on the content and method for merger notification procedures adopted by the Ministry.

626. In practice, the Agency also indirectly influences the notification of concentrations by issuing opinions on the request of undertakings or their proxies, who are in the dilemma of whether or not a transaction constitutes a concentration. If the conditions for notification of concentration are met, the Agency shall refer them to the obligation to submit a request for approval of concentration. Also, on the basis of information from the media, the Agency warns potential participants in the concentration about the obligation to submit a notification, under threat of punishment, i.e., a fine.

627. In accordance with the Agency's Tariff, the fee payable for a concentration filing depends on whether the concentration is cleared in Phase I or in Phase II. If the concentration ends up being approved already in Phase I, the fee is 0.03% of the aggregate annual turnover of the concentration participants generated in the year preceding the year in which the concentration is taking place, capped at EUR

596. *Id.*, Art. 52 para. 2.
597. *Id.*, Art. 52 para. 3.
598. *Id.*, Art. 52 para. 4.

15,000.[599] If the examination proceeds to Phase II and the concentration is ultimately or conditionality approved, the fee is 0.07% of the aggregate annual turnover of the concentration participants generated in the previous, capped at EUR 25,000.[600]

II. Turnover Calculation

628. As explained above, the relevant turnover of an undertaking is determined based on the total pre-tax revenue gained in the financial year preceding the year in which the concentration is taking place.

629. The Competition Act contains special rules for the calculation of turnover of undertakings engaged in the provision of financial, insurance, and reinsurance services. For banks and other financial institutions, the sum of the following items of income is used, after deduction of direct taxes related to them: (1) income from interest rates and similar income; (2) income from securities which includes: income from shares and other variable yield securities; income from participating interests in business entities and income from shares in affiliated business entities; (3) commissions receivable; (4) net profit on financial operations and (5) other operating income.[601]

630. For insurance companies that perform insurance or reinsurance activities, the total value of gross premiums, after the deduction of taxes and parafiscal contributions charged by reference to the amounts of individual premiums or the total volume of premiums.[602]

III. Market Share Calculation

631. There is no strict rule as to how the Agency calculates market shares when examining a concentration.

632. In general, the Agency calculates an undertaking's market share based on the data pertaining to sales, purchase, and/or production on the relevant market during the relevant period.

599. Tariff of fees of the Agency for Competition, Art. 2 para. 1 item 9.
600. *Id.*, Art. 2 para. 1 item 10.
601. Competition Act, Art. 51 para. 1 item 1.
602. *Id.*, Art. 51 para. 1 item 2.

IV. Other Relevant Notions

633. The parties to the concentration are obliged to suspend the implementation of concentration until the Agency adopts the decision approving the intended concentration or until the expiration of time limits for adopting the decision.[603] Exceptionally, the parties to a concentration may continue implementation of a takeover bid in accordance with the takeover legislation, provided that: (1) the acquirer does not exercise its voting rights after the subscription of the shares or (2) or does so only to maintain the value of the company taken over until the Agency issues the decision.[604]

634. In case of implementation of concentration without the approval of the Agency, the Agency may by means of decision adopt two types of measures: (1) order the disposal of acquired shares or participating interests in a company;[605] (2) prohibit or limit the exercise of voting rights in respect of the shares or participating interests in business entities by the parties to the concentration, and order to end the control of a joint venture or other forms of acquisition of control, which lead to prohibited concentration.[606]

§2. Structure of Proceedings

I. Preliminary Assessment and Full Investigation

635. The content of a notification of concentration is prescribed by the Guidance on the content and method for merger notification procedures adopted by the Agency. It prescribes that notification contains, *inter alia*, the following data and documents: (1) Basic data on merger participants (i.e., extract from the Central Register of Business Entities, certified statement of the natural person in case of achieving control over the undertakings to carry out merger on his behalf and for his account, etc.); (2) detailed description of the concentration type (i.e., manner of carrying out concentration, financial and other conditions and reasons for carrying out concentration, as well as ownership structure before and after carrying out declared concentration); (3) certified copy of act pursuant to which the concentration is carried out; (4) financial statement for undertakings which are participants in concentration, for the period of three years preceding the year when concentration is carried out; (5) data on number of employees of concentration participants in the last three years, including the year when the concentration is carried out; (6) data on five top purchasers/buyers and suppliers of each of the concentration participants in the last three years, including the year when the concentration is carried out; (7) data on financial value and scope of production and sale achieved by the concentration participants while selling goods or services at the relevant market in

603. *Id.*, Art. 56 para. 2.
604. *Id.*, Art. 56 para. 3.
605. *Id.*, Art. 58 para. 2 item 1.
606. *Id.*, Art. 58 para. 2 item 2.

Montenegro in the last three years; (8) evaluation of relevant geographic market and relevant product market and market share of concentration participant in the relevant market for the last three years before the application; (9) detailed description of the network of sale or distribution of goods and services of merger participants at the relevant market, production procedure, determination of prices and sale conditions; (10) analysis of business reasons for carrying out the concentration and anticipated effects to undertakings and to the relevant market.[607]

636. In practice, in the process of evaluating a request for approval of concentration, the Agency first starts from the submitted data and information in accordance with the requirements of the Guidance on the content and method for merger notification procedures, as well as determining the structure of the relevant market in accordance with the Rulebook on criteria for determining the relevant market. In the process of assessing the effects of concentration, the Agency also collects data from the competent state authorities and organizations, sector regulators, i.e., from competitors and potential competitors on the market.

637. The Competition Act stipulates that in the proceedings upon the request for issuance of the approval for implementation of a concentration, the Agency can adopt the following legal act:

(1) reject the request for approval of concentration if the conditions regarding notification and/or calculation of turnover are not fulfilled;[608]
(2) suspend the proceedings if the applicant withdraws the request;[609]
(3) approve concentration if by the appraisal of the effects determines that such concentration does not prevent, restrict or distort effective competition to a significant extent primarily by creating or strengthening a dominant position in the market;[610]
(4) approve concentration while ordering additional measures, conditions and obligations which must be complied with by the parties to the concentration prior to or following the implementation of the concentration;[611]
(5) reject the request if by the appraisal of the effects determines that such concentration would significantly impede effective market competition in the relevant market and particularly by creating a new dominant position or strengthening an existing dominant position.[612]

638. The Agency shall annul the decision approving concentration if the decision was taken on the basis of incorrect or false information and facts. In this case, according to the rules of criminal law, the issue of criminal responsibility for filing of incorrect or false information and facts can be raised.

607. Guidance on the content and method for merger notification procedures, Art. 2 para. 1.
608. Competition Act, Art. 56 para. 1 item 1.
609. *Id.*, Art. 56 para. 1 item 2.
610. *Id.*, Art. 56 para. 1 item 3.
611. *Id.*, Art. 56 para. 1 item 4.
612. *Id.*, Art. 56 para. 1 item 5.

639. The examination of a merger notification is exclusively performed by the Agency and can be divided in Phase 1 and Phase 2 stage.

640. If the Agency, on the basis of a completed notification of the concentration and other facts known to the Agency, estimates that it can be assumed that it does not have significant effects in the relevant market in terms of distortion of competition, such a concentration is considered permissible. In that case, the Agency will, without delay, notify the public of the admissibility of the concentration and issue it to the applicant decision on the approval of concentration. The Agency will clear a concentration in this phase without conducting an investigation.

641. Otherwise, if it is estimated that the implementation of the concentration could have a significant impact on competition in the relevant market, and especially if that is the case, concentration creates a new or stronger existing dominant position of the participants in the concentration, The Agency will issue a decision on the initiation of the procedure for assessing the admissibility of the concentration (Phase 2). Finally, at the end of Phase 2, the Agency adopts a resolution by which it clear or prohibit concentration.

II. Time Framework

642. The proceedings for the appraisal of a concentration shall commence on the date of receipt of a complete request for issuance of the approval for implementation of a concentration.[613]

643. In the process of evaluation of concentration, specific deadlines set by the Competition Act are applied. The Competition Act provides for different deadlines, depending on the decisions made by the Agency.

644. In the event that the Agency rejects the request for approval of concentration, if the conditions regarding notification and/or calculation of turnover are not met, or suspends the proceedings if the applicant withdraws the request, the time limit for adopting decision is twenty-five working days from the day of submitting the request.[614] If the Agency approves concentration, the time limit for adopting the decision is 105 working days from the day of submitting a complete request.[615] If the Agency approves concentration and orders additional measures which must be complied with by the parties, the timeline for adopting the decision is 125 working days from the day of submitting the request.[616]

---

613. *Id.*, Art. 55 para. 1.
614. *Id.*, Art. 62 para. 3 items 1–2.
615. *Id.*, Art. 62 para. 3 item 3.
616. *Id.*, Art. 62 para. 3 item 4.

645. However, the Competition Act does not contain a precise provision of the time limits for adopting the decision to approve a concentration when the Agency initiates the investigation (phase 2).

646. For the deadline for notification of concentration, *see* Part III, Chapter 3, §1 above.

III. Right of Defence

647. If the Agency assesses that the conditions for approval concentration are not met, it will send to the applicant a statement of objections with an invitation to respond within the deadline set by the Agency.[617]

648. Apart from responding to the statement of objection, the applicant is authorized to use other procedural rights, such as: seeking access to file, submitting briefs, requesting the holding of a hearing, requesting that certain data be protected, etc.

§3. Clearance and Conditional Clearance

I. Conditions and Undertakings

649. In its response to a statement of objection to the Agency, the applicant may propose additional conditions it is willing to accept, in exchange for a clearance.[618] If the Agency establishes that the proposed measures do not prevent, restrict or distort competition, it shall adopt the decision approving concentration. In the same decision, the Agency will order implementation of measures and time limits for the implementation, as well as the manner of control of the implementation of measures.[619] It is not prescribed by the Competition Act any limitation on the duration of the conditions.

650. The Agency will revoke the decision conditionally approving concentration if the parties to the concentration do not implement measures.[620] In this situation, as mentioned above, the Agency opens clearance ex officio. In the practice of the Agency, this has not happened so far.

651. It is not possible to submit an appeal against the final decision of the Agency. However, the interested party may challenge the decision in administrative dispute before the Administrative Court.[621]

---

617. *Id.*, Art. 57 para. 1.
618. *Id.*, Art. 57 para. 2.
619. *Id.*, Art. 57 para. 3.
620. *Id.*, Art. 57 para. 4.
621. *See* Part III, Ch. 4, §1 below.

§4. RELATION WITH OTHER MERGER CONTROL AUTHORITIES

I. Other Authorities with the Local Jurisdiction

652. It is explained in the text above, that some of the Montenegrin regulatory bodies have certain competences in the area of competition law, including their authority to approve concentrations in the sectors which fall under their jurisdiction.[622]

II. International Coordination

653. The Agency has signed general cooperation protocols with the authorities from Serbia, Croatia, Austria, Bulgaria, etc.

654. The Agency's 2017 Report shows that the Agency is in regular communication with the Delegation of the European Union to Montenegro. The Agency also communicates with the European Commission Directorate General for Competition.

622. *See* Part I, Ch. 2, §2 above.

Chapter 4. Challenging of the Administrative Decision

§1. Competent Courts

655. In accordance with the Competition Act, the Agency is responsible for initiating proceedings, conducting proceedings and issuing decisions in each individual case. The Agency's decisions on infringement are final in administrative proceedings. Decisions and conclusions adopted by the Agency may be challenged in administrative dispute before the Administrative Court.[623]

656. Jurisdiction and conduct of the Administrative Court are prescribed by the Law on Courts and the Law on Administrative Dispute (hereinafter 'LAD').[624] Law on Courts has a general norm which states that the Administrative Court shall decide in administrative disputes.[625] Also, the Administrative Court proceeds under the Law on Administrative Disputes which has similar norm which states that in an administrative dispute, the court decides on the legality of an administrative act and on the legality of other individual acts.[626] In matters of procedure that are not regulated by the LAD, the provisions of the law regulating the civil procedure are applied accordingly.

657. In an administrative dispute, the Court decides by a judgment or by a decision. By a judgment, the Court shall decide on a legal suit, and by a decision, the Court shall decide on procedural issues.[627]

658. In accordance with LAD, an administrative dispute may be started against an administrative or other act that has been passed in the second instance. An administrative dispute may also be started against an administrative or other act passed in the first instance, against which appeal is not allowed in an administrative or other procedure (which is the case in competition law issues).[628]

659. The Administrative Court has no specialized council for dealing with certain matters. In practice, cases are assigned to judges by the method of random allocation of cases according to the annual schedule of court jobs. The Administrative Court acts in all administrative areas against acts of state authorities. The first lawsuits in this area were filed in 2011 to the Administrative Court. The share of judgments in the field of competition law in the overall work of the Administrative Court is very low. For example, according to available data from 2011 to 2016, fifty disputes were launched, out of which seven were unresolved. This means that competition law issues are represented in only 0.035% of the total number of cases. Thus,

623. Competition Act, Art. 64.
624. LAD (*Zakon o upravnom sporu, Službeni list Crne Gore* 054/16).
625. Law on Courts, Art. 24.
626. LAD, Art. 2.
627. *Id.*, Art. 7 para. 1.
628. *Id.*, Art. 12 para. 1.

the lack of specialized councils, the number and scope of cases do not allow the court to establish a settled case law in this area.[629]

§2. Time Limits

660. An administrative dispute is started by a lawsuit. The lawsuit has to be submitted within twenty days as of the delivery of the administrative act to the party.[630] The complaint can be submitted to the Administrative Court directly, by post or email.

661. The lawsuit is delivered to the Agency for a response. The Agency is obliged to submit a reply within a time limit set by the Administrative Court, which may not be shorter than eight nor longer than thirty days. LAD does not contain a provision on the time limit for the Administrative Court to reach its decision.

§3. Scope of Judicial Review

662. A private or legal person who believes that some of his/her rights or legally based interests have been violated by an administrative or other act has the right to start an administrative dispute.[631] An administrative or other acts may be disputed: (1) in the case of breach of procedure;[632] (2) in the case of inaccurate and incomplete establishment of the facts;[633] (3) in the case of error of law.[634] In most cases in practice, plaintiffs include all three reasons in lawsuits.

663. In administrative disputes, the Administrative Court decides in an oral hearing or in a closed session. The Administrative Court will conduct an oral hearing if the party requests so in the lawsuit or in response to a lawsuit.[635] In an oral hearing, the chairman of the panel shall determine the day of the hearing and inform thereof the parties to the procedure and interested parties if any. The hearing may be postponed only for serious reasons, which shall be determined by the panel.

664. If the Administrative Court decides on a dispute in an oral hearing, it shall decide on the basis of facts established during the oral hearing and on the basis of facts established during the previous administrative procedure.[636] When deciding in a closed hearing, the Administrative Court may make a decision on the grounds of

---

629. Lakočević & Pot, *supra* n. 484, at 5.
630. LAD, Art. 17.
631. *Id.*, Art. 10.
632. *Id.*, Art. 14 para. 1 item 1.
633. *Id.*, Art. 14 para. 1 item 2.
634. *Id.*, Art. 14 para. 1 item 3.
635. *Id.*, Art. 28.
636. *Id.*, Art. 33. para. 1.

the facts established in the documents of the case. The Administrative Court examines the legality of a disputed administrative or other acts in the scope of the demand of a complaint.[637]

665. In accordance with the Constitution of Montenegro, the hearing before the court is public and the judgments are pronounced in public. Exceptionally, the court may exclude the public from the hearing or one part of the hearing for reasons of protection of morals, public order, for the protection of the private life of the parties, for the purpose of protecting military, business or official secret; and for the protection of the security and defence of Montenegro.[638]

666. Cases brought before the Administrative Court were heard by a panel of three judges (five judges in a request for a repeat of the proceedings). The Administrative Court shall decide by a majority of the votes of the panel.[639] A record of the deliberation and voting shall be kept and signed by the President, the members of the council and the court reporter. Deliberation and voting shall take place without the presence of the parties.[640]

667. The lawsuit is upheld or dismissed as unfounded by the judgment. If the lawsuit is upheld, the Administrative Court annuls the disputed act.[641]

668. When the court nullifies an act against which an administrative dispute has been started, the case shall be restituted to the condition in which it was before the nullified act had been passed.[642] If according to the character of the matter, which had been the object of the dispute, it is necessary to pass another act in place of the nullified administrative act, the Agency shall pass it without delay and at the latest within thirty days from the day of delivery of the judgment.[643] The Agency is bound by the legal concept of the court as well as by the remarks of the court with regard to the procedure.[644]

669. According to publicly available information, the Administrative Court of Montenegro issued a total of forty-one judgments in the period of 2012–2017. Out of them, twenty-seven judgments dismissing the lawsuit were filed against the Agency's decision and fourteen upholding the lawsuit. Judgments that uphold lawsuits in most cases relate to compliance with the rules of procedure, and not to a violation of substantive law.[645]

---

637. *Id.*, Art. 34.
638. Constitution of Montenegro, Art. 120.
639. LAD, Art. 37. para. 1.
640. *Id.*, Art. 37 para. 2.
641. *Id.*, Art. 35 para. 1.
642. *Id.*, Art. 56.
643. *Id.*, Art. 57 para. 1.
644. *Id.*, Art. 57.
645. Agency's Annual Report for 2017, p. 35.

670. In the previous practice of the Administrative Court, the subject of the assessment of the legality of the Agency's acts was related to procedural actions, periodic fines as well as the determination of competition violations. For example, until the adoption of the Competition Act, there was no legal basis for the Agency to review the impairment of competition by undertakings pursuing an activity of public interest that is why decisions of the Agency were held to be illegal by the Court. With respect to judgments reviewing the Agency's decisions on the periodic penalties of undertakings, the court has adopted lawsuits, holding that certain penalties are neither adequate nor properly determined because of misinterpretation of legal provisions. Acting upon the lawsuit of impairment of competition, the Court adopted judgments in which it upheld the Agency's reasons for the existence of impairment of competition. In a single case, the Court considered the right to exercise direct insight where it established the lawfulness of the Agency's procedure.[646]

671. The decision of the Administrative Court on the challenge of the Agency's decision is final and cannot be appealed.[647] However, against the final decision of the Administrative court the following extraordinary legal remedies may be submitted: (1) a request for reconsideration of a court decision (in Montenegrin: *zahtjev za ispitivanje sudske odluke*); (2) a request for a repeat of the procedure (in Montenegrin: *zahtjev za ponavljanje postupka*).[648]

672. The request for reconsideration of a court decision may be filed for the error of law and breach of procedure in the administrative dispute, which might affect the deciding on the matter.[649] The request for reconsideration of a court decision shall be decided on by the Supreme Court.[650] The request for reconsideration of the court decision has to be filed to the Supreme Court, within twenty days as of the day of delivery of the Administrative Court decision.[651]

673. The Supreme Court adopts or rejects the request for reconsideration of a court decision. In a judgment granting a request for reconsideration of a court decision, the Supreme Court may revoke or reverse the decision of the Administrative Court and set aside the impugned decision of the Agency.[652] If the Supreme Court revokes the decision of the Administrative Court, the case is referred back to the Administrative Court for a repeat of the procedure and decision. In the repeat of the procedure, the Administrative Court is obliged to carry out all procedural actions and to discuss issues referred to it by the Supreme Court.[653]

674. A request for a repeat of the procedure shall be filed if: (1) the party becomes aware of new facts or is able to use new evidence which could lead to a

646. *Id.*
647. LAD, Art. 8.
648. *Id.*, Art. 40 para. 1.
649. *Id.*, Art. 43 para. 1.
650. *Id.*, Art. 42.
651. *Id.*, Art. 44 para. 1.
652. *Id.*, Art. 47 para. 1.
653. *Id.*, Art. 47 para. 3.

more favourable outcome of the administrative procedure; (2) the decision of the Administrative Court occurred as a result of the criminal offence of a judge or a court employee; (3) the decision of the Administrative Court is based on a judgment rendered in a criminal or civil matter, which was subsequently overturned by another final court decision; (4) the document on which the decision of the Administrative Court is based is false or if the witness, expert witness or the opposing party, gave a false statement during the hearing before the court, and the decision of the court is based on that statement; (5) the party finds or acquires the opportunity to use an earlier decision of the Administrative Court rendered in the same administrative dispute; (6) the interested person was not given the opportunity to participate in the administrative dispute; (7) the judgment of the Administrative Court is contrary to the judgment of the European Court of Human Rights in the same matter.[654] A repeat of the procedure may be requested no later than thirty days after the date the party has learned of the reason for the repeat.[655] The Administrative Court shall decide on the repeat of the procedure in a panel of three judges.[656]

675. In proceedings, the question may be raised as to whether there is an obligation for the Administrative Court to stay the proceedings if a misdemeanour proceeding is initiated against the subject who initiated the administrative proceedings.

676. This was a common situation in practice. The Supreme Court answered this question in the rationale of the judgment on the request for reconsideration of a court decision in the case of Vodovod i Kanalizacija Budva. According to the Supreme Court, there is no obligation for the Administrative Court to terminate the administrative proceedings in this case since the final decision in the misdemeanour case is without prejudice to the administrative matter.[657]

---

654. *Id.*, Art. 48 para. 1.
655. *Id.*, Art. 49.
656. *Id.*, Art. 50.
657. Judgment of the Supreme Court of Montenegro No. 415/17 of 19 Oct. 2017, not available online.

Selected Bibliography

Andrea Marušić & Nikola Milović, *Competition policy in Montenegro,* 111–128 (Slavica Penev ed., Westminster Foundation for Democracy 2013).

Branislav Marović, *Ekonomska istorija Crne Gore* [*Economic history of Montenegro*] 425–664 (2018).

Branka Lakočević & Gordana Pot, *Analiza zaštite konkurencije u Crnoj Gori* [*Analysis of competition protection in Montenegro*], 4–5 (2016).

Dušanka Jauković & Slavica Bajić, *Ustavni sistem Crne Gore* [*Constitutional system of Montenegro*] 12–73 (2015).

Ivan Đekić, *Politika zaštite konkurencije u Srbiji – stanje i perspektive* [*Competition Policy in Serbia – State and Perspectives*], Ekonomske teme 229, 240 (2009).

Mijat Šuković, Three Different Constitutional arrangements of Montenegro, Journal for Constitutional Theory and Philosophy of Law 9, 43 (2009).

Mladen Vukčević & Miloš Bošković, *Judicial system in Montenegro – historical development, basic principles, and organisation*, Law & Justice Review 13, 26 (2016).

Nikola Milović & Mijat Jocović, *Impact of foreign direct investment on competitiveness of Montenegrin economy*, Transformations in Business & Economics 223, 230 (2017).

Nikola Milović, *Competitiveness and institutional framework for implementation of competition policy in Montenegro,* Economic themes 641, 654 (2010).

R. Radovanović, *Territorial Scope of Montenegrin Competition Law*, CEE Legal Matters, 63 (2017).

Snežana Miladinović, *Pravo za ekonomiste* [*Law for economists*] 160–165 (2012).

Željko Rutović, *Media Regulation in Montenegro*, Media dialogues, 7, 13 (2010).

Živko Andrijašević, *Istorija Crne Gore* [*History of Montenegro*] 24–202 (2015).

Selected Bibliography

Index

The numbers here refer to paragraph numbers.

Index

www.ingramcontent.com/pod-product-compliance
Ingram Content Group UK Ltd.
Pitfield, Milton Keynes, MK11 3LW, UK
UKHW021239300926
15471UKWH00013B/703